# Other books by Pastor Bim

- *31-Day Winning Wisdom Inspirational Guide for Women*

- *32 Enlightenment Nuggets for the Christian Married Woman*

- *The Marriage Care Manual*

- *Walking Along with God*

- *Obedience: The Daring and Determine Way to It*

- *By His Spirit*

- *Why Not with Jesus*

- *Biography of Bim* (coauthored with Damilola Okeke)

# POWER OF SEED

Pastor Bim Folayan

WESTBOW
PRESS®
A DIVISION OF THOMAS NELSON
& ZONDERVAN

WestBow Press books may be ordered through
booksellers or by contacting:

WestBow Press
A Division of Thomas Nelson & Zondervan
1663 Liberty Drive
Bloomington, IN 47403
www.westbowpress.com
844-714-3454

ISBN: 978-1-6642-2742-2 (sc)
ISBN: 978-1-6642-2741-5 (hc)
ISBN: 978-1-6642-2743-9 (e)

Library of Congress Control Number: 2021905285

Print information available on the last page.

WestBow Press rev. date: 04/27/2021

# Acknowledgments

My dear husband and all
partners of CET-c.
Nana, for the inspiration
in writing this book.
Banke, Dee, and Kemi, for your zeal.
Pastor Christina, for your commitment.

Seed to sow.
Sow to reap.
Reap to heap.
—Bim Folayan (2017)




Stop! Think!
What do you have that you were not given?
Some you sow, some you heap,
Release the seeds, for His reward to reap.
—Bim Folayan (2018)

## Psalm 112:3–9 (NCV)

Their houses will be full of
wealth and riches,
and their goodness will continue forever.
A light shines in the dark for honest people,
for those who are merciful
and kind and good.
It is good to be merciful and generous.
Those who are fair in their business
will never be defeated.
Good people will always be remembered.
They won't be afraid of bad news;
their hearts are steady because
they trust the Lord.
They are confident and will not be afraid;
they will look down on their enemies.
They give freely to the poor.
The things they do are right
and will continue forever.
They will be given great honor.

To the God of all Wisdom. Psalm 113.

# Contents

# Introduction

As long as the earth continues, planting
and harvest, cold and hot, summer and
winter, day and night will not stop.
—Genesis 8:22 (NCV)

We give and we receive; we sow and we reap; planting must continue so that the harvest will be unceasing. Because day and night never stop, the harvest is guaranteed for all planting done on good soil.

We sow our time and effort in the work we do for the harvest of income. When no planting has been invested, reaping becomes far-fetched. The hand that sows must reap. Sowing can be in any form. It can be a gesture or a special sacrifice. Sacrifice implies investing the extra and additional endeavor, which may be difficult and painful. I remember how, in 2011, God told me to be of service to another woman of God, and persecution ensued, but through it, God did not leave me uncared for (Isaiah 41:10 AMP). Today, this investment is yielding its dividend. The uncomfortable sacrificial service may be long-term or short-term, it may be perpetual or temporary, but it is invariably to our advantage (Psalm 126:5–6).

God commands a tenth of our harvest or income. He commands that we be responsible for "meat" in His storehouse, which we must honor. This is our duty because we are God's children and automatic partners with God our Father in kingdom business. We ensure there will be means or funds to run His will on earth for all people to come to His saving grace.

God is good; He's asked the giver to prove or challenge His faithfulness and see if He will not pour out so many blessings that we wouldn't have room to contain them (Malachi 3:10–11). God's blessing and provision come in diverse means beyond financial provision. What money cannot deliver; God can provide.

And God is able to make all grace
[every favor and earthly blessing]

come in abundance to you, so that you may always [under all circumstances, regardless of the need] have complete sufficiency in everything [being completely self-sufficient in Him], and have an abundance for every good work and act of charity. (2 Corinthians 9:8 AMP)

# Chapter 1

# The Nature of Giving

He gave himself as a payment to free all people.
—1 Timothy 2:6 (NIV)

Jesus gave everything, including Himself, in order to redeem us from sin unto God. He gave and gained us. The power in giving causes us to receive. God gave His only begotten to redeem the whole world back to Himself.

God provides us with seeds. The Bible says He gives seed to the sower (Isaiah 55:10); only those who sow seeds receive harvests. Jesus was a type of seed that yielded harvest or redemption of souls headed for destruction. "Who gave himself for us, that he might redeem us from all iniquity, and purify unto himself a peculiar people, zealous of good works" (Titus 2:14). When a seed is sowed, it leaves the hand of the sower, it is buried, and then it dies. Nonetheless, it does not remain dead. It springs into life, grows, and brings forth many other seeds. Hallelujah!

"Verily, verily, I say unto you, Except a corn of wheat fall into the ground and die, it abideth alone: but if it die, it bringeth forth much fruit" (John 12:24). God wants us to sow so that we may reap. He has given every person a means as seed. No human is empty. All Moses had was just his rod, but God did a lot with it. God said to Moses in Exodus 4:17 (NCV), "Take your walking stick with you, and *use it* to do the miracles." If Moses had nothing else, He had the walking stick. God has not left anyone without a means. Our gesture also counts as seed. You can offer kindness; even your smile can give hope to someone. Sow, and motivate a generation. Jesus said in Matthew 25:40 (NIV), "Whatever you did for one of the least of these ... you did for me."

If you sow, you must reap. Reaping is harvesting what has been sowed or cultivated. Sowing in this regard is to invest or to give up something, whereas reaping is to receive or to harvest the reward or the produce of sowing. Anything can be sowed or invested, such as our time, money, assistance, and help. If you invest your time in good diet and good exercise, for example, you will reap the fruit of good health and fitness. If you also invest or give up something on God's instruction, you will reap God's reward for obedience and enjoy more of His grace, favor, and closeness that qualified Abraham as God's friend.

This is God's Word in Isaiah 58:10–12.

> And if thou draw out thy soul to the hungry, and satisfy the afflicted soul; then shall thy light rise in obscurity, and thy darkness be as the noon day:
>
> And the Lord shall guide thee continually, and satisfy thy soul in drought, and make fat thy bones: and thou shalt be like a watered garden, and like a spring of water, whose waters fail not.
>
> And they that shall be of thee shall build the old waste places: thou

shalt raise up the foundations
of many generations; and thou
shalt be called, The repairer of
the breach, The restorer of paths
to dwell in.

Have you made investment sowing recently
or some time ago, or are you planning to? If
not, cultivate the thought and plan a seed
time. The Bible lets us know in Ecclesiastes
3:2 that there is a time to sow and a time to
harvest. Planting and reaping are essential
to Christian living. Authentic Christianity
points us to minding the need of others. A
child of God must live a generous life as God's
channel/transistor of blessing to a needy
world. "For the poor shall never cease out of
the land: therefore I command thee, saying,
Thou shalt open thine hand wide unto thy
brother, to thy poor, and to thy needy, in thy
land" (Deuteronomy 15:11).

God blesses us so we can be a blessing. We
are His conduits. Psalm 24:1 tells us that
the earth and everything in it are the Lord's.
We are stewards of funds in our possession.
God owns all. These blessings come to us
for God's purpose. We therefore must seek to

fulfill His purposes in line with His will for what He has blessed us with. Luke 4:4 tells us, "Man shall not live by bread alone but by every Word of God." This means that people must operate according to God's will and direction. God's will is for us to replenish the earth with the good we reap from it. We consequently must sow so we can harvest more of what is invested. We sow when we meet the needs around us.

On the other hand, to live by bread alone is to live for self and things that matter to us. God's way encourages our supportive action of giving to charitable good causes. Doing this make our lives count and relevant in God's kingdom because of the lives we affect through our selfless actions.

Times do arise when it's a struggle to give up a seed and sow it because of the feelings to keep it. Nonetheless, doing the will of God amounts to wisdom. "Let each one give [*thoughtfully and with purpose*] just as he has decided in his heart, not grudgingly or under compulsion, for *God loves a cheerful giver*" (2 Corinthians 9:7 AMP; emphasis mine). God's promises of recompense for the sower or giver is certain. The giver, in the process of his gesture, is being instrumental to establishing God's will on earth. His gesture serves as God's answer to the prayer of the needy, causing glory and testimony to the name of the Lord. Psalm 126:5–6 states,

> They that sow in tears shall reap in joy. He that goeth forth and weepeth, bearing precious seed, shall doubtless come again with rejoicing, bringing his sheaves with him.

Moses had something God could use. Do you have what God can use too? Do you have anything significant God could use? Invest and sow it because it is needed to replenish and serve God's will on earth. Whatever we make available will be valuable in serving others and fulfilling God's purpose. After Moses's willingness, the Bible then refers to Moses's rod as "the walking stick of God" (Exodus 4:20 NCV). Invariably, Moses's ordinary rod became extraordinary. It became blessed. Hence, it was upgraded to be a means or source of blessing simply because it was made available.

Even Moses's availability resulted in higher abilities for him. He yielded himself to be used of God. The more our activities and services are of impact in any God-given circumstance, the more effective result we produce. This is due to the potency of our input. The power or the effectiveness of our seed of action is what generates the fruits of our harvest. At times the fruits, rewards, and outcome transcend the giver or sower just as we see in the life of Abraham, whose harvest exceeded many generations after him. "Through your descendants all the nations on the earth will be blessed, because you obeyed me" (Genesis 22:18). God made this profound promise to Abraham. What legacy are we also leaving through personal sacrifices?

Genuine life of abundance is blessing traceable to life of generosity. Abraham passed God's test of selflessness over the only child we had waited so long to have, and he did not fail God. He reasoned that everything came from God. He was wise to remember that God is the source of Isaac and that if God gave him Isaac, then He can be trusted to give again. The reward of Abraham's action is recorded for us in Genesis 12:2, where God said to him, "And I will make of thee a great nation, and I will bless thee, and make thy name great; and thou shalt be a blessing." Furthermore, in Genesis 13:16, God said to him, "And I will make thy seed as the dust of the earth: so that if a man can number the dust of the earth, then shall thy seed also be numbered." He is the God of abundance (Ephesians 3:20).

Abraham's selflessness is an example to us. He did not live focused on earthy possessions but was God focused. Even God wondered whether He could do a thing without telling Abraham (Genesis 18:17). He passed God's test at Moriah (Genesis 22:1–18). His altruism impressed God, and he qualified as God's friend (Isaiah 41:8). Consequently, God blessed Abraham. He became a channel of God's blessing, his seed (generation) with Him. Are you a seed of Abraham? Then you also are a channel of God's blessing.

Our prerequisite nature must exhibit this outstanding quality of our forefather Abraham. Genesis 18 tells of his very hospitable and generous nature. In verse

7 (GNT), the Bible records it was done to a high-quality standard, even to strangers. "Then he ran to the herd and picked out a calf that was tender and fat, and gave it to a servant, who hurried to get it ready." Unknowingly, he hosted God! What a wise opportunity! Abraham was so willingly generous that he set up himself and his wife for God's special blessing. Even when Sarah laughed, God overlooked it. Abraham had impressed God with his faith, and blessings of a lifetime ensued.

Abraham's selfless quality implied that he didn't have to know who the three strangers were, but he was kind to them. He was sensitive to their needs. He was self-sacrificing toward them. His giving and magnanimous nature launched him into realization of his uttermost heart's desire coupled with generational blessings for his household. Hebrews 13:1–2 enjoins us to "let brotherly love continue. Be not forgetful to entertain strangers: for thereby some have entertained angels unawares."

Encouraging generosity, Exodus 36:2–7 gives another account of a profound giving nature.

And Moses called Bezaleel and Aholiab, and every wise hearted man, in whose heart the Lord had put wisdom, even every one whose heart stirred him up to come unto the work to do it: And they received of Moses all the offering, which the children of Israel had brought for the work of the service of the sanctuary, to make it withal. And they brought yet unto him free offerings every morning. And all the wise men, that wrought all the work of the sanctuary, came every man from his work which they made; And they spake unto Moses, saying, The people bring much more than enough for the service of the work, which the Lord commanded to make. And Moses gave commandment, and they caused it to be proclaimed throughout the camp, saying, Let neither man nor woman make any more work for the offering of the sanctuary. So the people were restrained from bringing. For the stuff they

had was sufficient for all the work
to make it, and too much.

This is the nature of God. Our God is generous
in all things, in love and in mercy. He fed
the Israelites with Manna from heaven daily,
and with more than enough on the sixth
day so they do not have to gather on the
seventh day, which has been declared holy
and for their rest. He gave us heaven's best
in the person of His dear Son, Jesus Christ.
The giving of His only Son, Jesus Christ,
was a seed gesture that brought many sons
to God's saving power. Just like the Father,
Jesus gave. He gave Himself up as the perfect
sacrifice that redeemed humans back to
God. He died a cruel death to safe the souls
of those who were undeserving. He was the
Seed of God who died, was buried, and then
rose for the harvest of souls to the life of
God. Determined to save us, He laid off His
glory, dying to self to save humans. He said
to God the Father, "Lo, I come, to do thy will
O God" (Hebrews 10:7). No person needs to
die for another. Jesus paid the ultimate price
by His sacrifice for all. That is generosity at
its peak.

God made humans and gave them His very nature, even the nature of giving and generosity. God's Word teaches us to be kind-hearted and generous toward one another (Philippians 2:3). In His Word, He says to love our neighbor, be our brothers' keeper, and ensure it is well with them. "Yes indeed, it is good when you truly obey our Lord's command, 'You must love and help your neighbors just as much as you love and take care of yourself'" (James 2:8 TLB). Our generous gesture toward others are seeds and investment that are worthy of heaven's reward and harvest. By the nature of God in us (Genesis 1:27 and 1 John 4:17), Hebrews 13:16 enjoins us, "And do not forget to do good and to share with others, for with such sacrifices God is pleased."

Our obedient corresponding actions to God are worthy seeds. Seeds are either tangible or incorporeal. They are incorporeal because they might not be physical or bodily but spiritual. It might not be visible to the naked eye but a form of expenditure with tangible cost. Everything we do as humans is accounted for. Every action has its value. What we sow is what we reap. Jeremiah

32:19 says, "For thine eyes are open upon all the ways of the sons of men: to give everyone according to his ways, and according to the fruit of his doings." The gesture of Rebecca toward Abraham's servant earned her a handsome reward. She went the extra mile in giving service of kindness to Abraham's servant that brought her into the blessing of Abraham's family, becoming his daughter-in-law (Genesis 24).

"Now he that ministereth seed to the sower both minister bread for your food, and multiply your seed sown, and increase the fruits of your righteousness" (2 Corinthians 9:10). A seed is one of many seeds in a fruit. When sowed, a single seed yields multiple fruits or harvests. A seed has the power and potency of duplicating itself in multiple harvest. The Bible state in Luke 6:38, "Give, and it shall be given unto you; good measure, pressed down, and shaken together, and running over, shall men give into your bosom. For with the same measure that ye mete withal it shall be measured to you again." This spans over forgiveness, generosity in kindness, provision of aid and support for the needy, and other charitable acts. These are worthy seeds born out of the nature of God. Because seeds produce after its kind, our seeds of charity and philanthropy can be targeted toward specific goals. If we sow kindness, we reap kindness; if we sow forgiveness, we reap forgiveness. The Lord's prayer states, "Forgive us our trespasses as we forgive those who trespass against us" (Matthew 6:14). It implies that what we sow is what we reap. Abraham's generosity toward God with his son Isaac earned him the father of many nations. Tabitha sowed kindness and service to the people (Acts 9:36–43), and her gesture prevented her death when the people rushed for Peter that she must not die.

Seeds have inherent power to reproduce. Those in God's will prosper (Deuteronomy 30:9). Their seeds and anything related to them flourish (Psalm 1:3). Reward and harvest are generated from investments. They are fruits generated from our seed or labor. God's Word in Psalm 92:12 tells us that the righteous will flourish. The wise turns their seeds around through the investment action of sowing that corresponds with God's principles. Seeds sowed on the right soil will germinate and produce a harvest.

God is our source of seeds, and our sowing must follow His course. Seeds sown on the right soil with the right nutrients and other components for healthy growth of the seed yield the harvest. You cannot sow wrongly and expect returns. Our motives are known to God, who cannot be deceived; He is the bringer of these harvests in due season. If we sow rightly, we earn rightly.

By sowing wisely and with discernment of God's will for us, we circumvent sowing ignorantly in the wrong soil that does not produce results. We must be discerning! A farmer won't plant on a patched and unfertile sandy soil and expect a harvest. Ignorance is not an excuse. If your seed does not hit the right soil, it misses its harvest! You cannot give your tithe to just anyone you see at the door of your church and rush off, expecting that person to drop it in the church offering bag while you await the blessing. If your offering has not targeted God's project but sits in the wallet of the person you handed it to, you will be wrong to await harvest. In this case, the giver's attitude is unwise and is to blame for the action. When you have given to God the wise way, you can await harvest. What the church admin does with it is between them and the God you have obeyed, who promises to bless the righteous (Psalm 35:27). Seeds from a good heart and source with God's purpose bring super blessings.

There are times we even sow into (invest in or make a sacrifice for) a blessing or something we admire, appreciate or respect. What we do here is, we attract or provoke the harvest of such a blessing by our seed, investment or input in such. In Matthew 10:40–42, the Bible mention the prophet's reward: "He that receiveth you receiveth me, and he that receiveth me receiveth him that sent me. He that receiveth a prophet in the name of a prophet shall receive a prophet's reward; and he that receiveth a righteous man in the name of a righteous man shall receive a righteous man's reward. And whosoever shall give to drink unto one of these little ones a cup of cold water only in the name of a disciple, verily I say unto you, he shall in no wise lose his reward."

Consider the quality of your seed, and do according to your ability or based on the conviction received of God. The widow who fed Elijah and was massively blessed was convinced. The result of good attitude (2 Corinthians 9:7), good seed, and good soil is bountiful. This is one reason why it is so vital to follow divine direction when planting (Proverbs 3:5–6). As God's offspring, He guides us. He knows all things and sees all things. Scripture tells us in Isaiah 55:8–9 that His thought and ways are not like ours but are higher than our own ways and thoughts. It implies that He does not see things the way we see things, because He is supreme. He warned prophet Samuel against anointing Eliab, David's brother, who had the kingly charisma and panache (1 Samuel 16:6–7). God's choice was young shepherd David.

In Malachi 3:10 (NLT), God's Word states "'Bring all the tithes into the storehouse so there will be enough food in my Temple. If you do,' says the Lord of Heaven's Armies, 'I will open the windows of heaven for you. I will pour out a blessing so great you won't have enough room to take it in! Try it! Put me to the test!'" Storehouse implies God's house where His Word (food to our spirit) is served and ministered. It is a place of worship, where our spirit is nourished. This is God's establishment, and there should not be lack in it. God has commanded us therefore to ensure the supply. This responsibility is given us to our own benefit, and the same scripture also challenges to prove and test it.

If we remember that everything belongs to God, then we ask ourselves why we should be disobedient with 10 percent of what is His. Why keep away from doing the will of the real owner, God? We are mere custodians! Remember Jesus warning His disciple against selfishness with the story of an egocentric man in Luke 12:15–21? "After all, we brought nothing with us when we came into the world, and we can't take anything with us when we leave it" (1 Timothy 6:7 NLT). We therefore must honor God with our substance, with what He's blessed us with (Proverbs 3:9). Abraham proved altruism, passing God's test by his willingness to release to God what belongs to Him. He remembered the source of Isaac. He was wise to consider the Giver of Isaac. The Bible recorded that Abraham believed God to provide. The reward of his obedient action was generational blessings. God even called him friend because it takes benevolence to know a true friend. Are you a friend of God? "Let them shout for joy, and be glad, that favour my righteous cause: yea, let them say continually, Let the Lord be magnified, which hath pleasure in the prosperity of his servant" (Psalm 35:27).

In wisdom, it is pivotal to invest our seeds where God finds it vital and causes a harvest. Wisdom is availing ourselves of seed time, whereby we release the seeds irrespective of the pain associated with letting go. A key factor is time, the period and duration of waiting for good returns. One of the fruits of the spirit mentioned in Galatians 5:22 is patience. We require it while our seed is maturing for harvest. The Living Bible translation states, "But when the Holy Spirit controls our lives he will produce this kind of fruit in us: love, joy, peace, patience, kindness, goodness, faithfulness." If we do not lean on our understanding, sense knowledge, or human understanding; How productive a man will be if ruled, controlled, and guided by the Spirit of God, who directs our seed and prepares us a harvest. "You have all wisdom and do great and mighty miracles; for your eyes are open to all the ways of men, and you reward everyone according to his life and deeds" (Jeremiah 32:19 TLB).

Each seed has its imminent power to reproduce, multiply, and reproduce for greater outcome. Instead of planting, if we keep what God sees as seed, we deprive ourselves of multiplicity. As God's children, we live by His Spirit and divine principles. People have lived by worldly precepts, hence losing relationship with God. Some have wrecked relationships with families and good friends, forgetting that some of the things that they see as valuable today will be worthless in some time to come. The Bible enjoins us thus:

> Lay not up for yourselves treasures upon earth, where moth and rust doth corrupt, and where thieves break through and steal: But lay up for yourselves treasures in heaven, where neither moth nor rust doth corrupt, and where thieves do not break through nor steal. (Matthew 6:19–20)

Your seed has got to fall on the right soil for it to produce the right result. You simply do as the Word of God directs and as the Spirit of God will have you. Release your service, offering your time and talents and doing according to what Proverbs 3:27 (NIV) enjoins us: "Do not withhold good from those to whom it is due, when it is in your power to act." Giving liberates from the bondage of stinginess, which is never the nature of God. Givers don't lack. Let God's blessing flow through you. Let someone be blessed and helped and then praise and adore God because of you. The more you give, the more you serve as conduit of God's channel of to those in need (2 Corinthians 9:8). Let the light and life of God shine, alleviating lack, pain, and suffering. "Let your light so shine before men that they may see your moral excellence and your praiseworthy, noble, and good deeds and recognize and honor and praise and glorify your Father Who is in heaven" (Matthew 5:16 AMPC).

The reward of corresponding action to needs around us is numerous and cannot be overemphasized. We see one of such in Isaiah 58:10 and 2 Corinthians 9:6, which underpins the popular saying that what you sow is what you reap. The farmer plants seeds from his good fruits to produce more of the same. Our invested seeds regenerate after their kind. A seed is defined as the unit of reproduction of a flowering plant, capable of developing into another such plant.

Every seed sown has a waiting period between sowing and bearing fruits. Patience is one of the fruits of righteousness. As children of God, must exhibit this trait and nature. Patience is a great virtue and an adorable quality. Perseverance is an attribute associated with winners because winners do not quit but press on and press in. Prevailing circumstances do not distract or deter them. They are self-motivated and convinced about their purpose.

Patient people can be called purposeful. They are focused because they are resolute. They persevere till the see results, and with God on their side, the end shall surely and eventually justify their means.

When planted, some seeds take a few weeks or months before we see the harvest. Some take even longer depending on the nature and type of seed. The quality of our seed is important to God. It must be good and with the right attitude. Quality seed produces quality harvest. Cain's sacrifice was rejected by God because it was lacking in quality. "By faith Abel offered unto God a more excellent sacrifice than Cain, by which he obtained witness that he was righteous, God testifying of his gifts: and by it he being dead yet speaketh" (Hebrews 11:4). God is moved by our investment and sacrifice. The widow's mite (very small copper coins) touched Jesus and moved Him to testify of her. Her seed, though comparatively small, was all she had. Jesus acknowledged her in Luke 21:1–4 (NKJV).

> And He looked up and saw the rich putting their gifts into the treasury, and He saw also a certain poor widow putting in two mites. So He said, "Truly I say to you that this poor widow has put in more than all; for all these out of their abundance have put in offerings for God, but she out of her poverty put in all the livelihood that she had."

When a seed that is sowed leaves the sower, and its departure implies its "death," which is what happens to a seed in the soil. With time it germinates into a plant that invariably produces multiply seeds and harvest for the sower. God's Word states in John 12:24, "Verily, verily, I say unto you, Except a corn of wheat fall into the ground and die, it abideth alone: but if it die, it bringeth forth much fruit."

## Chapter 2

# Being a Blessing

And God is able to make all grace abound toward
you; that ye, always having all sufficiency in
all things, may abound to every good work.
—2 Corinthians 9:8

God's Word in Revelation 3:8 (CEV) came to
me: "I know everything you have done. And
I have placed before you an open door that
no one can close. You were not very strong,
but you obeyed my message and did not deny
that you are my follower."

In 2007, I committed to running the ministry
God had given me to women. I ran this
assignment with income from my secular
job, and in 2009, by faith I resigned the
job, using my residual income and personal
facilities to continue to fund the commission.
I was oblivious of other support at the time

but only aware and driven by the fact that God had commissioned me to giving support to women and marriages. I persevered the challenge of running the ministry by faith. The results, encouraging feedbacks and words from beneficiaries were enhancing; one that was particularly motivating is, "No vision from God lacks His provision and no assignment from God lacks His consignment." This phrase boosts my hope.

The Word of God in Galatians 6:9 encouraged me. It states, "And let us not be weary in well doing: for in due season we shall reap, if we faint not." My goal was seeking Him to do His will. Despite the pressure and strain I faced, I was convinced that my diligence to His will was sure to pay off in the long run. Each step of the way, I hoped in God, the Author and Finisher (Hebrews 12:2), believing that if He started it, He would see me through (Philippians 1:6).

I remember one day at my place of work a few weeks before launching out into full-time ministry God had spoken the scripture in Matthew 10:8 me, "freely have you received, freely give," and I think I understood what

God meant.I began the assignment using my residual income and my savings, running the ministry in and out of the United Kingdom for over a year. I ran conferences, seminars, and monthly forums for women in several locations that were entirely free of charge.

I waited on God for the appointed time to request external supported. I had obeyed and I had sowed. It was time. It was clear that it was time to involve people who had shown interest in the ministry projects. I did not have to do any convincing; the hand of God they saw on the assignment was enough. People eagerly participated financially. A dear woman of God called me on phone and told me that God had asked her to do something for the ministry, she gave monthly financial support. I remember a big fan, Nana, who went about seeking support for the group out of her own freewill, and she inspired my writing this book.

Nana had no paid employment at the time and therefore had no earnings. She had been part of the group for some months and was fascinated by the ministry's projects. She was full of zeal, spreading the word about the work of CET-c for Women. The moment God permitted financial contributions from others into the work, she would look for means in order to make her contribution. She would encourage her friends to give to the work. Full of zest with joy, she would encourage those slacking not to delay in supporting the vision.

I believe this can only be an act of God. Nana's devotion was amazing. She was self-driven, and this zeal can only be attributed to divine inspiration. Her selflessness in seeing that the ministry is financial enhanced caused me to reflect on God's faithfulness: "Him that is able to do exceeding abundantly above all that we ask or think, according to the power that worketh in" (Ephesians 3:20). But God did not leave Nana unrewarded. I write this book, *Power of Seed*, about eight years after I was inspired by her action. Within this period, I counted it a privilege to witness God's faithfulness and fulfilment to her personal dreams and goals.

> One person gives freely, yet gains even more; another withholds unduly, but comes to poverty.

A generous person will prosper; whoever refreshes others will be refreshed. (Proverbs 11:24–25)

God honors our seed of obedience to His will (Psalm 111:5 NIV). Also, in Proverbs 27:18 the Bible tells us, "Whoso keepeth the fig tree shall eat the fruit thereof: so he that waiteth on his master shall be honoured."

Having "kept the fig tree" by what was sowed, it was necessary to wait on the Lord of harvest (Matthew 9:38) to give the harvest by multiplying what was sown. The period of waiting on God for harvest requires patience and dependence on God. He alone makes harvest possible.

While we remain unwavering in our walk with God and full of hope in Him alone, we can be guaranteed the harvest. The Bible states in Proverbs 23:18 that the expectation of the righteous shall not be cut off. God is generous to the generous. He proves His faithfulness to the faithful. He never leaves those who hope in Him hopeless. God can do beyond our imagination (Ephesians 3:20). If we have been faithful and prove our confidence in

Him, the Bible tell us that hope does not make us ashamed. God will show up for the one who has applied his heart to giving, for the giver will be given, and the sower will reap. Luke 6:38 enjoins us to give so it is given back to us in good measure. Do not allow misleading thoughts and misconception or someone's bad experience cheat you from the benefits of honoring kingdom principles on giving. Search God's mind for you, see what He's put in your heart to do, and do it.

Apply God's wisdom ("seek His wisdom," James 1:5). Avail yourself of the opportunity of service to the Lord, because He "is able to make it up to you by giving you everything you need and more so that there will not only be enough for your own needs but plenty left over to give joyfully to others" (2 Corinthians 9:8 TLB). Be Word-driven, not fleshly driven, in this kingdom gesture. God reaches the world through us. We are His means, for His use and purpose. He gave His best to redeem us, and we therefore give to redeem others. It demands a sacrifice of our means to reach out to others with the gospel. Our lives must count, and they must serve as seeds so they may produce a God kind of harvest. Jesus was a seed, so we ought to be too. We are God's channel of blessing to the world.

The Bible refers to us as vessels of honor, which means a conduit or vehicle that the Helper uses in fulfilling His purposes here on earth. Everything we own belongs to God; the earth and everything in it are His (Psalm 24:1). We do ourselves the honor and advantage of giving. When we make our means—what we own and what we do—facilitate God's processes on earth or in the lives of others, we become a blessing. Good gesture is always a ladder to good returns.

> Don't ever forget kindness and truth. Wear them like a necklace. Write them on your heart as if on a tablet. (Proverbs 3:3 (NCV)

Support good causes and give purposefully, for what you sow, you reap. Your giving is your security. It comes back when you most required it. Givers don't lack. The seeds you have sowed justify your recompense. The Bible says that God makes all things beautiful in His perfect time. Help will show up when it is most appropriate (by God's standard). Therefore, friends, do not be afraid to give. The giving has power: it liberates and instils the spirit of liberty and abundant life that Christ produced for us.

> The thief comes only in order to steal and kill and destroy. I came that they may have and enjoy life, and have it in abundance [to the full, till it overflows]. (John 10:10 (AMP)

Jesus was a means by which God restored humankind to Him. When Jesus had completed His task here on earth, He said He was leaving us another comforter (John 14:16), exactly like Him, in the form of the Holy Spirit. The Holy Spirit helps communicates God's will to us. He helps us to fulfill God's will. And as God's children, we are here in the world as His agent of blessing. We are the means by which certain prayers offered to Him are answered. When God wants to execute answer to the prayer of someone in need, He communicates it to one of His own who will be faithful to perform according to His will and direction.

Giving is an act of service and demonstration of support, interest, kindness, and love. The Bible states in 1 John 4:8 that God is love. Love gives. To know God is to give because it is His nature to give. We therefore can make giving intentional and a lifestyle.

Hospitable giving got the Shunammite woman a son. When the son died, the seeds of her gesture cause the harvest of her son back to life" (2 Kings 4:17, 32–37), just as Tabitha's giving raised her to back to life (Acts 9:36–42). Our Lord Jesus, during His day, had compassion on people and always, He reached out to them and helped (Matthew 15:29–39). He did not stop at just being sorry or sympathetic—He backed his empathy with action.

In the tenth chapter of the book of Acts, Cornelius's seeds yielded a harvest of salvation for his entire household.

> There was a certain man in Caesarea called Cornelius, a centurion of the band called the Italian band, A devout man, and one that feared God with all his

house, which gave much alms to the people, and prayed to God always. He saw in a vision evidently about the ninth hour of the day an angel of God coming in to him, and saying unto him, Cornelius. And when he looked on him, he was afraid, and said, What is it, Lord? And he said unto him, Thy prayers and thine alms are come up for a memorial before God. And now send men to Joppa, and call for one Simon, whose surname is Peter: He lodgeth with one Simon a tanner, whose house is by the sea side: he shall tell thee what thou oughtest to do. And when the angel which spake unto Cornelius was departed, he called two of his household servants, and a devout soldier of them that waited on him continually; And when he had declared all these things unto them, he sent them to Joppa. ...

Now while Peter doubted in himself what this vision which he had seen should mean, behold,

the men which were sent from
Cornelius had made enquiry
for Simon's house, and stood
before the gate, And called, and
asked whether Simon, which was
surnamed Peter, were lodged
there. While Peter thought on the
vision, the Spirit said unto him,
Behold, three men seek thee. Arise
therefore, and get thee down, and
go with them, doubting nothing:
for I have sent them.

Then Peter went down to the men
which were sent unto him from
Cornelius; and said, Behold, I am
he whom ye seek: what is the cause
wherefore ye are come? And they
said, Cornelius the centurion, a
just man, and one that feareth
God, and of good report among
all the nation of the Jews, was
warned from God by an holy angel
to send for thee into his house,
and to hear words of thee.

Then called he them in, and lodged
them. And on the morrow Peter

went away with them, and certain brethren from Joppa accompanied him. And the morrow after they entered into Caesarea. And Cornelius waited for them, and he had called together his kinsmen and near friends.

And as Peter was coming in, Cornelius met him, and fell down at his feet, and worshipped him. But Peter took him up, saying, Stand up; I myself also am a man. And as he talked with him, he went in, and found many that were come together. And he said unto them, Ye know how that it is an unlawful thing for a man that is a Jew to keep company, or come unto one of another nation; but God hath shewed me that I should not call any man common or unclean.

Therefore came I unto you without gainsaying, as soon as I was sent for: I ask therefore for what intent ye have sent for me?

And Cornelius said, Four days ago I was fasting until this hour; and at the ninth hour I prayed in my house, and, behold, a man stood before me in bright clothing, And said, Cornelius, thy prayer is heard, and thine alms are had in remembrance in the sight of God.

Send therefore to Joppa, and call hither Simon, whose surname is Peter; he is lodged in the house of one Simon a tanner by the sea side: who, when he cometh, shall speak unto thee.

Immediately therefore I sent to thee; and thou hast well done that thou art come. Now therefore are we all here present before God, to hear all things that are commanded thee of God.

Then Peter opened his mouth, and said, Of a truth I perceive that God is no respecter of persons:

But in every nation he that feareth him, and worketh righteousness, is accepted with him.

The word which God sent unto the children of Israel, preaching peace by Jesus Christ: (he is Lord of all:) ...

While Peter yet spake these words, the Holy Ghost fell on all them which heard the word.

And they of the circumcision which believed were astonished, as many as came with Peter, because that on the Gentiles also was poured out the gift of the Holy Ghost. For they heard them speak with tongues, and magnify God. Then answered Peter, Can any man forbid water, that these should not be baptized, which have received the Holy Ghost as well as we? And he commanded them to be baptized in the name of the Lord. Then prayed they him to tarry certain days.

This account about Cornelius is rather intriguing. It was recorded that he honored and reverenced God; he was a devout man. He was generous in alms giving. He was God's answer to people's need. His laudable gesture caused for praises to God from the needs met through him. Consequently, he earned the opportunity to experience the Holy Spirit (verses 44–48) and extended salvation to people beyond his immediate family in the process (verses 28, 34–36) because of his generosity. First Corinthians 6:17 (AMP) states, "God loves a cheerful giver [and delights in the one whose heart is in his gift]." Good gestures evoke blessings for the giver. The giver will enjoy favor with God and humankind.

Let God use what you have. Our seed becomes a memorial in the heart of the receiver and produces thanksgiving to God. The Bible states in Matthew 5:16, "Let your light so shine before men, that they may see your good works, and glorify your Father which is in heaven."

The church in Thessalonica received earned apostle Paul's prayer because of their seed of hospitality. "With this in mind, we constantly pray for you, that our God may make you worthy of his calling, and that by his power he may bring to fruition your every desire for goodness and your every deed prompted by faith" (2 Thessalonians 1:11 NIV). Paul said this of them in verse 3, "We are bound to thank God always for you, brethren, as it is meet, because that your faith groweth exceedingly, and the charity of every one of you all toward each other aboundeth." Kindness between the believers impressed and inspired Paul to pray for the brethren.

Whatever we sacrifice or invest in others will certainly return to us as great harvest. God gave His very best to us for our redemption (His harvest). God honors our labor of love to support others. His Word assures recompense, stating that in all labor there is profit, that the laborer is worthy of his wage. In Hebrews 6:10, it is stated, "God is not unjust; he will not forget your work and the love you have shown him as you have helped his people and continue to help them."

God gave, and having His nature, we therefore also give. It is the core of our existence, to replenish the earth with our substance (Genesis 1:28). Seed reproduces, so we must sow by being a blessing to others. Christ Himself gave up (as a seed) to redeem the lot of us. Consequently, we must distribute His love through sharing the seed of His good news (Mark 16:15). The Bible refers to us as the salt and light of the world. We are carrier and distributor of flavor and taste and of direction to the world. As God's children, giving to the world is not optional. We give and tell the gospel to the world.

There is this saying: "Whatever you make happen for others, you make happen for yourself." How true this is! I therefore prophesy, "There is someone who has always unselfishly supported the work of God. You are so much yielded to supporting others. Grace and honor is about to locate you. Undoubtedly, you will attract favor and the blessings of Spirit of God behind the work you have supported—saith the Spirit of God."

God made each of us unique such that we can be blessings to the world with our uniqueness. There is something we each deliver and share. Giving is not restricted to money and presents; it extends to as simply as a smile, compliment, encouraging words, giving support, a hand of assistance, and numerous other helpful gestures. Adam and Eve nurtured the garden and cared for the animals there, which was the world around them. What is your world? It starts with your immediate environment. How are you making an impact? Do not search too far or ask how. First think of how a single person can be blessed because of you. It may cost you something, but it is worth it. It may be painful or hectic, but it is a great thing to be a blessing. Sowing maybe not be easy, but be sure of harvest, which is always sweet. The pain of sowing is soon forgotten when the joy of harvest sets in. Planting may be tedious, but there is such joy to have a harvest. When harvest comes for some fruits, it drops all around. The same await the sower who understands the opportunity in each seed sowed. "They that sow in tears shall reap in joy. He that goeth forth and weepeth, bearing precious seed, shall doubtless come again with rejoicing, bringing his sheaves with him" (Psalm 126:5–6).

Putting our faith in God's Word is a prerequisite for a successful and fulfilling Christian life. Psalm 84:12 (NIV) says, "Lord Almighty, blessed is the one who trusts in you." Abraham, the father of faith, pleased God because of his exceptional trust in God. The Bible tells us in Romans 4:3 that God counted it as righteousness for Abraham. The Bible records that the blessing and reward of his confidence in God transcended his generation: "The promise comes by faith, so that it may be by grace and may be guaranteed to all Abraham's offspring ... but also to those who have the faith of Abraham" (Romans 4:16 NIV). This includes the believers. Galatians 3:29 states, "And if ye be Christ's, then are ye Abraham's seed, and heirs according to the promise."

By Abraham's willful sacrifice, he inherited the promise of God. You can attain God's plan for your life by trusting this same God with what you own in your custody, for He owns all things. Psalms 24:1 tell us, "The earth is the Lord's, and the fulness thereof; the world, and they that dwell therein." Abraham did not delay or hesitate in the instruction to sacrifice Isaac. He recognized the source of Isaac. Abraham was focused in strict compliance with God's directives. He was determined and punctual. He did not hold back from the Owner and Maker of all things, the Provider and Giver of Isaac. Abraham demonstrated trust and confidence in God by His timely and determined response.

By obedience we avail ourselves of outcomes that build us in deeper trust and confidence in God from level to level and from glory to glory. Just like how from Isaac to the patriarchs and the nation of Israel and beyond, Abraham became the father of many nations.

It was through faith, trusting God that Abraham inherited God's promise. He was patience, waiting on God. Similarly, seeds will undergo divine processing to return as fruits. When there isn't faith, then there is fear (of losing). Focus on being a blessing, for your labor is not in vain. Galatians 6:9 says, "And let us not be weary in well doing: for in due season we shall reap, if we faint not."

I remember God asking me to give in support of a ministry. This is without the ministry soliciting. I obeyed by setting up a monthly plan from my personal account. Months later, God said to increase it to an amount far and above my monthly giving to my own ministry. This made me wonder, but I did not consider it necessary to question it, because I knew God must have a plan. I faithfully and joyfully gave to this ministry month in and month out. Before long, I begin to experience in my own ministry the same special blessing that I admired in this other ministry.

Good soil will give good harvest. The Bible tells us in Deuteronomy 8:18 that God is the one who gives power to get wealth. By wisdom and insightfulness, you sow on a good soil. Reach out to others from God's perspective by being His channel of blessing. Extend benevolence and aid to those in need. See people with God's eyes, and don't be kind only to people who are kind to you or never offended you. Build an acceptance of others because it is a form of generosity with good harvest. You could have been in a situation where your act of kindness ended up in discouragement. Do not be frustrated or allow discouragement to deter your blessing.

There is a harvest of blessing in waiting for each seed of gesture.

Holding on to mundane things is carnality. Don't allow greed, selfishness, or self-centeredness cheat you of a future of unending harvest. Whatever good you do to others comes back to you. Good gestures are like ladders you prepare ahead of the time it will be required when climbing to where you want to be. It is a vehicle to special assets. It is a bed prepared by you for how you want to lie down. It is a means of preparing a future of harvest.

The Bible says without faith, it is impossible to please God, and those who come to God must believe that He is the Rewarder of those who diligently seek Him (Hebrews 11:6). There is a period of waiting after seed sowing before harvest arrives. Every seed of generosity yields after itself and a door to other blessings.

Seeds can germinate only under the right soil and conditions. God's Word instructs us to apply our hearts to wisdom. Ensure you do not fall victim of scam or undue pressure to give. Check the motive and be certain within your heart that your action is within the acceptable and perfect will of God. Divine insight and true peace and conviction is required for productive giving. Please God and not human. If God is in it, be steadfast in action. Your seed is your future. It is your security.

Disappointment and discouragement of the past must not hinder you from being a blessing to others. The Bible lets us know that discouragement is of the devil. We see in John 10:10 that he has come to kill, steal, and destroy. If your generous or good gesture seems to have been destroyed, discouraged, or frustrated, do not allow the devil to get you stuck you in that rut, thereby stealing future blessings from you. Overcome his scheme to make you self-centered. Derive motivation from God's Word in Luke 6:38, which says, "Give, and it shall be given unto you; good measure, pressed down, and shaken together, and running over, shall men give into your bosom. For with the same measure that ye mete withal it shall be measured to you again."

In Malachi 3:8–12, God asked us to meet the need for running His house (church) so that there isn't lack in His temple, where He is worshipped. We cannot afford not to make a return to Source. The Word of God from His house builds us and liberates, so we must keep it running and effective through our individual contributions and inputs. God is our Giver and Provider, and we must not be victims of stinginess, which is of Satan, who would rather steal than give.

Fear of lack and depletion makes people hoard and not give; hence they are constricted within the limits acknowledged by their mindset. Romans 12:2 tells about renewing our minds and not conforming to world standards and sensory perceptions. Trust in God. Be supply conscious, not lack conscious. The Bible gives account of a boy in John 6:1–14 who could see beyond his lunch. In verse 14, his action glorified God. He offered his lunch where Jesus ministered to the crowd. He did not withhold it but gave it up so it could be a blessing to others. His seed was sowed, and it had to be buried and to die (i.e., the period it left his hand), but it returned in multiplied harvest! It fed five thousand men (not counting women and children) with twelve baskets leftover!

Matthew 16:8–10 (NIV) states, "Jesus asked, 'You of little faith, why are you talking among yourselves about having no bread? Do you still not understand? Don't you remember the five loaves for the five thousand, and how many basketfuls you gathered? Or the seven loaves for the four thousand, and how many basketfuls you gathered?'" He is a God of multiplication. Whatever we give up in faith, He returns in multiple folds. The Bible state in James 4:17, "To him that knoweth to do good, and doeth it not, to him it is sin." Give with discernment. Give with conviction of God's will based on Proverbs 3:5–6 so you do not gratify the flesh (yourself and humankind). Give with discretion, allowing God to direct you into His perfect will.

What you give may leave your hand but does not leave your future. Your giving inspires divine provocation of blessings and the goodwill of humankind. The Bible states, "Then you will find favor with both God and people, and you will earn a good reputation. Trust in the Lord with all your heart; do not depend on your own understanding. Seek his will in all you do, and he will show you which path to take" (Proverbs 3:4–6 NLT).

God owns the earth and everything in it (Psalm 24:1), but He requires you for multiplicity to release like the little boy in the book of John 6. This principle also applies same way to our proceeds that God has blessed us with. Malachi 3:10–12 enlightens us about the power behind our 10 percent. In certain instances, to provoke more, more is sowed and given by faith and personal conviction. Take the case of a widow's sacrifice and obedience that resulted in drastic and unceasing blessing (1 Kings 17:8–16). "For God is not unrighteous to forget your work and labour of love, which ye have shewed toward his name, in that ye have ministered to the saints, and do minister" (Hebrews 6:10).

If you have just read this and feel you wish to obey God regarding giving, an important warning is to not give up on yourself. There is hope for you to be a happy and generous giver. The best way to change is to embark on change. Be intentional about laying down your sacrifice regardless of internal or external opposing forces. Refuse to compromise due to bad experiences all around but simply play your part in kingdom advancement and the furtherance of the gospel of Christ. Execute the power of seed with the goal of obeying God, and look to Him alone to meet your own need. Thousands have spared their lives beyond their possessions for the sake of sharing the gospel and salvation that you have today.

# Chapter 3

# Our Great Shepherd

That great shepherd of the sheep.
—Hebrews 13:20

David said in Psalm 23:1 that the Lord is his Shepherd, and hence he shall not want for supply. The same Shepherd that leads to green pastures also leads by directing us to where to sow so we may reap the harvest that meet our needs. Our seed produces effects that regenerate because it's based on the direction of the great Shepherd, for God cares and cradles our plans when we put our plans in His bigger plan for us.

Be sure to put your trust in God's almighty ability. As you do, He will handle what matters to you. Ensure that you "trust the Lord with all your heart, and don't depend on your own understanding. Remember the Lord in all you do, and he will give you success" (Proverbs 3:5–6 NCV). When you give, don't give to only those who are able to recompense you in return. God gave us Jesus Christ despite the fact that we cannot pay back His sacrifice. This is true giving. We therefore must emulate Him, the Shepherd of our souls. "The steadfast love of the LORD never ceases; his mercies never come to an end" (Lamentation 3:22).

As our great Shepherd guides us on to green pastures, we must follow even if we do not yet understand or know His full plan. When He asks us to sow, though we wonder and ponder, we do it because He never leads astray. "He maketh me to lie down in green pastures" (Psalms 23:2). His full plan and harvest are sure to be revealed in due season. He says in John 10:27, "My sheep hear my voice, and I know them, and they follow me."

God is a God of harvest, a faithful Shepherd. He will not lead is astray. He said in John 10:4–5 that His sheep (His offspring) know (can discern) His voice from that of a stranger. For His children to receive His supply and blessings, they must obey His Word (both written and spoken) directing them to the green pasture (right and fertile ground).

Giving liberates us from stagnation. It takes the Great Shepherd to lead us where the pasture is green. God asked Isaac to remain in Gerar. The Bible tells us that Isaac sowed in a land that suffered famine (Gerar), and he prospered (Genesis 26:13–14). Indeed, the blessing of God makes one rich (Proverbs 10:22). When the good Shepherd guides you, operate in truth and not ignorance. For He is the truth and life (John 14:6). He is the light of the world (John 8:12) to guide us into all truth. He guided Isaac into His reality.

> "And the Lord appeared unto him, and said, Go not down into Egypt; dwell in the land which I shall tell thee of:
>
> Sojourn in this land, and I will be with thee, and will bless thee; for unto thee, and unto thy seed, I will give all these countries, and I will perform the oath which I sware unto Abraham thy father

And I will make thy seed to multiply as the stars of heaven, and will give unto thy seed all these countries; and in thy seed shall all the nations of the earth be blessed;

Because that Abraham obeyed my voice, and kept my charge, my commandments, my statutes, and my laws.

And Isaac dwelt in Gerar." (Genesis 26:2–6)

Isaac obeyed.

Abraham, Isaac's father, also obeyed God, which translated to generational divine guidance. When things did not add up, these two obeyed. My dear reader, let God be God by being in charge over our lives.

Giving stiffens and frustrates the spirit of lack. Poverty and lack are broken by resisting the life of insufficiency and limitations caused by spirit of fear; The fear of depletion from giving. Givers don't lose. They understand that they are investing through sowing. They know that what they have given awaits their future. They understand God's principle of giving in Luke 6:38. God's children have His blessings as they administer His Word. He rewards their ministration (giving). He calls us to give for His work in Malachi 3:8–12. He is called the Rewarder of those who diligently seek Him (Hebrews 11:6), who do not reason as the world but rather by the Word. Romans 12:2 states, "And be not conformed to this world: but be ye transformed by the renewing of your mind, that ye may prove what is that good, and acceptable, and perfect, will of God." This means changing the way we think about giving so that it implies subtraction. He wants us to renew our minds in hope and trust of His faithfulness to replenish.

In Hebrews 12:2, Jesus disregarded the heavy price He had to pay on the cross, for the harvest of mankind. "Looking unto Jesus the author and finisher of our faith; who for the joy that was set before him endured the cross, despising the shame, and is set down at the right hand of the throne of God." We never lose by giving; instead, we defeat and dominate the spirit of fear, limitation and timidity that hounds us.

Like God did for Abraham, sometimes when He wants to bless, He checks our faithfulness, selflessness and confidence in Him. Abraham proved not greedy. He was insightful of God's blessings toward him and in turn was generous, even to strangers. Like him, we must be mindful that everything belongs to God, the world and everything it consists of (Psalms 24:1), the gold and the silver, the cattle upon a thousand hills (Psalm 50:10). God owns everything.

Why is it sometimes difficult to let go? First Corinthians 4:7 (TLB) states, "What are you so puffed up about? What do you have that God hasn't given you? And if all you have is from God, why act as though you are so great, and as though you have accomplished something on your own?" Wisdom is doing the needful and allowing God's direction. God channels His blessing to the one who will in turn be a distributor. The result of Abraham's selflessness and trust in God brought him harvest that outlived him (Genesis 22:1–18).

The sacrifice of Jesus for our salvation was not because we qualified or merited it. It was an act of seed sowing that has yielded redemptive harvest of believers saved by God's grace (unmerited favor). God gave regardless. In the Father's nature, our generosity should extend to the undeserving. The Bible tell us that God loved us while we were yet sinners (Romans 5:8). "For ye know the grace of our Lord Jesus Christ, that, though he was rich, yet for your sakes he became poor, that ye through his poverty might be rich" (2 Corinthians 8:9). This is God's demonstration of self-sacrifice.

Yield to God and trust Him. He leads and directs in ways that allow us to channel His blessings to others. He will keep you (the conduit) nourished so that you are daily supplied. As He routes His supplies through you to those in need, and as they get served and nourished, you serve as embodiment of His faithfulness. "God loves the person who gives happily. And God can give you more blessings than you need. Then you will always have plenty of everything—enough to give to every good work" (2 Corinthians 9:7–8 NCV).

Embrace the great Shepherd's guardianship, which leads to eternal verities such that you never want for harvest. Let Him guide you on how to sow, where to sow, and when to sow. Submit to Him. Be fully yielded to Him. Do not lean on your own understanding. Let Him direct your path. "Trust in the Lord with all thine heart; and lean not unto thine own understanding. In all thy ways acknowledge him, and he shall direct thy paths" (Proverbs 3:5–6). For He gives power and direction to get wealth (Deuteronomy 8:18).

Because He is the Creator and Provider of seeds (Isaiah 55:10), it is wise to surrender to His directions. The Bible states in Proverbs 4:7 that wisdom is the principal thing, enjoining us to get this most imperative and foremost essential of life. Compliance to God is wisdom. Obedience pays. Abiding in God's Word means that you are thoroughly furnished with power over situations and circumstances. It's a principle that works.

I have come to be steadfast with obedience because it pays off in the long run. God is good and would only instruct on the path of goodness irrespective the cost because it is for our good. Therefore, out of respect and reverence for His supremacy, we must obey. The fear and reverence of God is the beginning of wisdom, because as you go through uncompromising execution of His will, you become wise. The fear of God is the starting point of divine wisdom.

Daniel had an excellent spirit because of the fear of God in him. He reverenced and acknowledged God in all His ways, respecting and regarding His Word. He honored and submitted to God in all his ways despite opposing forces, even in the face of death. He would rather be unpopular but steadfast in God's instructions.

No wonder that Daniel operated in extraordinary intelligence and strength, being able to do exploits (Daniel 6:3). The force of wisdom from his commitment and deep-rooted dedication to God exalted and promoted him (Daniel 6:26). The Bible supplies us knowledge of God's Word so we are thoroughly furnished with God's wisdom, encouragement, and ability. "All scripture is given by inspiration of God, and is profitable for doctrine, for reproof, for correction, for instruction in righteousness: That the man of God may be perfect, thoroughly furnished unto all good works" (2 Timothy 3:16–17). We gain wisdom and insight through the Word of God written for our benefit.

We realize that it wasn't God intention to take Isaac from Abraham but to check and secure Abraham's faithfulness toward Him. But Abraham did not withhold God's gift, Isaac. Rather, he portrayed confidence in Jehovah Jireh (God the Provider), who is able to provide another and much more. He is the God over everything (Luke 1:37). Abraham's confidence in God earned him blessings that transcended several generations after him (Genesis 26:4).

Exodus 34:20b states, "None of you are to appear before Me empty-handed." Malachi 3:10 indicates that God is honored when we come before Him with gifts that demonstrate thoughtfulness toward Him and His Word. If we desire the blessings that God gives, then we must also be eager to display generosity in response to His will.

God's Word teaches generosity through being selfless with just 10 percent of what God has provided us. God's direction trains us in the path of righteousness and right living that makes us fulfill the law of supernatural blessings by which we may remain in abundance and constant supplied. "I will give you great harvests from your fruit trees and fields, and never again will the surrounding nations be able to scoff at your land for its famines" (Ezekiel 36:30 NLT).

Recently, the Lord ministered to me that our seeds are like arrowheads: they shoot us to where we want to be. That is, they facilitate and enhance progression and secure our goals.

Many years ago, I was working for an affluent organization in Africa that provides its staff an annual lump sum as housing allowance upfront. I was receiving mine on the first anniversary of my employment. Later that same evening was mid-service with a call to be a blessing to a mission project in foreign currency. I was convinced that I knew what I needed to do, and I did it. It was several years later that I got the insightfulness that my action of many years back had jolted my foreign relocation.

The psalmist in Psalm 35:27 states, "Let them shout for joy, and be glad, that favour my righteous cause: yea, let them say continually, Let the Lord be magnified, which hath pleasure in the prosperity of his servant." God is keen to reward diligence done in His name.

Some time ago, I invested in caring for a young chap through his court ordeal. He returned to show appreciation to the charity I run. He embarked on monthly giving to the ministry. A few years down the line, as a result of his seed, he did what no youth of his age had ever done in his county, and he enjoyed the support of his local council in his enterprise by way of motivating other youths. Today, his business is well established along with ongoing support of his local authority. Indeed, no one gives to God and His work and is short-changed.

About the time I went into full-time ministry in 2009, I met a lady at a women's conference. I think I had met her once before, and on this second occasion, the Lord nudged me to present a new shirt I had gotten for myself and cherished. I barely knew this lady, but I made efforts to follow it through. Our relationship moved from acquaintances to friends. A few months down the line, she began to play major support roles in ensuring I was well established in ministry. She is married to a pastor and supplied major equipment for my programs; she even loaned me her choir at these initial stages. It was as if God had planned with her. My simple seed of just a shirt got me access to facilities and opportunities that far outweighed the cost of my shirt. It became a privilege for me to have sowed.

There are diverse seeds. God has given to everyone a measure of seed (e.g., a service or gesture), just as the Word has it in Romans 12:3b that God has given each of us a measure of faith. It is the same for seed that translates to fruits or multiple seeds. No one is short-changed. Moses had a rod and did something with it. A young lady in my ministry opened up her home (a basic flat) as a meeting venue, to serve as a branch of a charity in her area. Several months later,

God provided her a dream home, spacious and beautifully furnished. Glory to God! "Though thy beginning was small, yet thy latter end should greatly increase" (Job 8:7). This young lady's act proved Psalm 37:4, which says, "Delight thyself also in the Lord: and he shall give thee the desires of thine heart."

The story of Cain and Abel portrays that God rewards benevolence. "Now Abel kept flocks, and Cain worked the soil. In the course of time Cain brought some of the fruits of the soil as an offering to the Lord. And Abel also brought an offering—fat portions from some of the firstborn of his flock. The Lord looked with favor on Abel and his offering" (Genesis 4:2–4 NIV). Similarly, the young chap I mentioned earlier earned God's favor. He returned with his sheaves with him (Psalm 126:6). He came back to also meet the need of the ministry, availing himself as God's response to the ministry—hence His reward. As First Corinthians 15:58 states, "always abounding in the work of the Lord, forasmuch as ye know that your labour is not in vain in the Lord"

Will a man rob God? Yet ye have robbed me. But ye say, Wherein have we robbed thee? In tithes and offerings. Ye are cursed with a curse: for ye have robbed me, even this whole nation. Bring ye all the tithes into the storehouse, that there may be meat in mine house, and prove me now herewith, saith the Lord of hosts, if I will not open you the windows of heaven, and pour you out a blessing, that there shall not be room enough to receive it. And I will rebuke the devourer for your sakes, and he shall not destroy the fruits of your ground; neither shall your vine cast her fruit before the time in the field, saith the Lord of hosts. And all nations shall call you blessed: for ye shall be a delightsome land, saith the Lord of hosts. (Malachi 3:8–12)

This blessing of provision, supply, protection, and abundance accompanies those who gives of their substance as scripture stipulates. In return for their generosity, God provides them increased seeds for further blessings and harvest. "And prove me now herewith, saith the Lord of hosts, if I will not open you the windows of heaven, and pour you out a blessing, that there shall not be room enough to receive it" (Malachi 3:10). Because of this reason, the Bible enjoins us to give joyful with praise and thanksgiving (1 Chronicles 16:29) in cognizance of God's faithfulness.

As our funds go into gospel projects and investment, we make food or funds available for God's storehouses. The power of seed must not be underestimated. David set us a huge example. Nothing God gave him mattered more to him than God and His instructions. He was a selfless, self-sacrificing giver and sower (2 Samuel 24:20–25). By insightful understanding, he recognizes that all that humans possess belong to God (Psalms 24:1), so he knows not to hesitate but to be generous to God and His cause.

Giving can serve as an effective tool of evangelism as we reach out to the needy. It will also translate to productivity in the life of the giver (Isaiah 58:7–12). When we give, we do it in service, obeisance, and honor of the Provider. Giving destroys the yoke of poverty. It liberates from the spirit of stagnation behind lack. It is to our own advantage that we give. Givers don't lack. The Bible tells us that God is unwilling to do without a cheerful giver whose heart is toward being a blessing to others.

Let each one [give] as he has made up his own mind and purposed in his heart, not reluctantly or sorrowfully or under compulsion, for God loves (He takes pleasure in, prizes above other things, and is unwilling to abandon or to do without) a cheerful (joyous, "prompt to do it") giver [whose heart is in his giving].

And God is able to make all grace (every favor and earthly blessing) come to you in abundance, so that you may always and under all circumstances and whatever the need be self-sufficient [possessing enough to require no aid or support and furnished in abundance for every good work and charitable donation].

As it is written, He [the benevolent person] scatters abroad; He gives to the poor; His deeds of justice and goodness and kindness and benevolence will go on and endure forever! (2 Corinthians 9:7–9 AMPC)

God trusts such people as His channel of blessing to supplication made by others. He therefore keeps them in health (Isaiah 58:8), constantly supplied and productive (Luke 6:38), causing them to remain fruitful because they are fountains of blessings sensitive to needs around them. He trusts them not to close their eyes and hearts to the needs around them.

If you feel that need to sow a seed and are wondering how, because you are unsure, be happy for the giving nature of the Father in you (John 3:16). Let the spirit gain dominion over the flesh, give of your substance. For happy are you because you are a means to a need. God loves a cheerful giver. "Every man according as he purposeth in his heart, so let him give; not grudgingly, or of necessity: for God loveth a cheerful giver" (2 Corinthians 9:7). Give and leave the receiver with God to deal with if you become unsure. The Bible says it is more blessed to give than to receive. At least, you won't have cheated yourself of the blessing tied to that act of sowing. Our seeds in the soil of other people's lives causes a memorial with the receiver in thanksgiving for your act and with God in blessings to you. God is glorified, and the giver is edified. The prayer of thanksgiving of the receiver waters the seed of the giver as his praise to God abounds in harvest of further blessings to both parties.

Second Corinthians 9:10–12 (AMP) describes this outcome.

> Now He who provides seed for the sower and bread for food will provide and multiply your seed for sowing [that is, your resources] and increase the harvest of your righteousness [which shows itself in active goodness, kindness, and love]. You will be enriched

in every way so that you may be generous, and this [generosity, administered] through us is producing thanksgiving to God [from those who benefit]. For the ministry of this service (offering) is not only supplying the needs of the saints (God's people), but is also overflowing through many expressions of thanksgiving to God.

Rely on God (Proverbs 3:5–6; Isaiah 26:3–4). He is dependable. His Spirit in us is the best thing that happens to humans. By the Holy Spirit we are guided (John 14:26). The Psalmist calls Him his Shepherd (his Jehovah Rohi) who leads to the right pastures (Psalm 23). This is who He is to you if you are born again (born of Him). Otherwise, refer to the last two pages of this book.

Seek the Great Shepherd for direction on where to sow. If you must wait till you are sure so you are convinced, please do. Note that recompense is not always financial. The result comes in different shapes and forms.

Only be guided by God's Spirit. If He says to wait, then wait. Holding on doesn't mean you are not doing anything; it's an action taken to wait or seek God for confirmation. But when you have it, go for it—don't delay. Beware of undue excuses, which will amount to your disobedience which deters reward and blessings. Sow your seed, be generous, wait for God and trust for Him to act.

> My soul, wait thou only upon God; for my expectation is from him. He only is my rock and my salvation: he is my defence; I shall not be moved. (Psalm 62:5–6)

# Chapter 4

# Harvest

Now unto him that is able to do exceeding
abundantly above all that we ask or think,
according to the power that worketh in us.
—Ephesians 3:20

Are you sowing on the right soil? If you are
unsure, seek the Lord in prayers for direction.
Jeremiah 29:12 (NIV) states, "When you will
call upon me and go and pray to Me, and
I will listen to you." Depend on God, who
gives profitable direction instead of relying
on your own rational. "Trust in the Lord with
all your heart. Never rely on what you think
you know. Remember the Lord in everything
you do, and he will show you the right way"
(Proverbs 3:5–6 GNT). Be attentive to God
and follow His will. The right soil will aid
good growth and harvest.

The Father remembers and rewards seed sowing and acts of sacrifice or generosity. Sowing (giving) in any form results in blessings from God (2 Corinthians 9:11). Implying that God blesses the vessels He uses. From Peter's boat, Jesus ministered to the crowd. Peter's boat had served Jesus, and in return he got the catch of his life.

> And it came to pass, that, as the people pressed upon him to hear the word of God, he stood by the lake of Gennesaret, And saw two ships standing by the lake: but the fishermen were gone out of them, and were washing their nets. And he entered into one of the ships, which was Simon's, and prayed him that he would thrust out a little from the land. And he sat down, and taught the people out of the ship.

> Now when he had left speaking, he said unto Simon, Launch out into the deep, and let down your nets for a draught.

And Simon answering said unto him, Master, we have toiled all the night, and have taken nothing: nevertheless at thy word I will let down the net.

And when they had this done, they inclosed a great multitude of fishes: and their net brake.

And they beckoned unto their partners, which were in the other ship, that they should come and help them. And they came, and filled both the ships, so that they began to sink. (Luke 5:1–7)

How awesome! Generosity pays! In verse 3, Peter gave up his boat. Verse 4 launches the reward of Peter's generosity. In verses 6 and 7, he reaped beyond his widest expectation.

God guides and gives discernment and discretion to His children on what, when, where, and how to sow. It is a privilege to be God's conduit of supply to His projects on earth and to people in prayer petitions to Him, and for Him to make His own children be answers to such requests. God is not pleased with anyone selfish or grumpy with giving. He wants us to be our brothers' keeper, love our neighbors as ourselves, and be merciful to others the way He has been to us. James 2:8 (TLB) states, "Yes indeed, it is good when you truly obey our Lord's command, "You must love and help your neighbors just as much as you love and take care of yourself." Nehemiah was selfless in building the wall of Jerusalem, and he gave opportunities to fellow Jews in this laudable project. He knew not to fail God. He was focused despite opposition (Nehemiah 6:1–16).

God loves, takes pleasure in, prizes above other things, and is unwilling to abandon or do without a cheerful, joyous, prompt giver whose heart is in his giving (2 Corinthians 9:7 AMP). Like Nehemiah, be focused. Do not be discouraged. What is important is availing yourself the opportunity of God's blessings and reward, for the one who has not sowed cannot expect harvest. Check out the following scriptures: Isaiah 54:10–12, Hebrews 10:35–36, Isaiah 61:7 (TLB), and Psalm 41:1–2.

Bear in mind that God is not unrighteous to forget your labor of love (Hebrews 6:10). He will not ignore our seed gesture but rather, He will cause it to bear fruits for you. We see it in the case of Cornelius in Acts 10:4, when God sent His angel to him, saying, "Thy prayers and thine alms are come up for a memorial before God."

I was privileged to have information on Nana's reward. Her liberality to the ministry had paid off. Though we had lost touch, I was privy to news of her harvest. Serving as a pediatric nurse in the early days of my ministry to the work of God in my hands, with her unfettered generosity in the year 2010 had produced her returns! God's blessings abounded to her and her family a hundredfold. Several promotions had taken place for her and her household over the years. A major family aspiration had come to pass. Hearing about her progress for me was great honor and opportunity. It was no surprise to me as such because I know God is faithful. To whom I ascribe all the glory. As a wise "farmer," she had sowed and watered despite her deprived circumstance in order to provoke multiple timely family harvests, hence proving 2 Corinthians 9:7 (AMP).

Giving opens uncommon doors. I remember years back when my daughter had a language exchange program with a student from France, whom I had hosted for a week as my own child. I had made special preparations for this student to make his time enjoyable, comfortable, and memorable. I had stretched my budget, and a day or two afterward, I received a call from a retiree lady that she was visiting. When she came over, it was with an envelope enclosing a sum of money for me. I was taken aback and quite hesitant, because it was quite a sum she had in the envelope for me. She honored my curiosity for her action. She told me that the Holy Spirit had prompted her, insisting that I should not be hesitant and should embrace her gesture. It was such a laudable gesture. I appreciated her obedience and communicated to her that her action was timely. I was awed by this supernatural supply. I valued the lady's diligence and acknowledged God's faithfulness. In one way or another, today I am a witness to her harvest. The Lord had arranged the fruits of her seed far ahead, all she needed then was to initiate it by acting on His instruction which she did. Today, her seed had grown and matured, and her harvest, which I am party to, has been a continuous one. This is like fruits whose harvest are not just for a season, but are perennial, who keep yielding fruits throughout their lifespan. At God's ordained time, this lady's harvest showed up. Indeed, God is committed to His promise on reward and recompense (Galatians 6:9). "For the Son of man shall come in the glory of his Father with his angels; and then he shall reward every man according to his works" (Matthew 16:27).

I was also privileged to witness Dee's harvest. God is truly faithful. Everything we do and sacrifice in His name gets duly rewarded. But the time and season of recompense, He alone decides. Dee gave all the care, support and assistance to her pastor in moving home; few months down the line, God moved Dee from a run-down apartment to an elegant home in a prime location.

Let your life count: invest in sowing with the aim of being an answer to a need. Focus on the Father's will. Proverbs 19:17 says, "He that hath pity upon the poor lendeth unto the LORD; and that which he hath given will be pay him again." Harvest awaits every seed sowed righty. The sacrifice of sowing is worth the harvest. The investment labor in planting is appreciated when its returns come. Trust in God is required through sprouting to fruiting. So, you may well enjoy the season of planting now, keeping it watered with hope in a rewarding God.

The Holy Spirit guides us into harvest. When He wants to bless us, He might require us to do the unusual so that we can get the uncommon. This may involve planting the remnant or what is left, to secure the harvest of more, just as in the case of the widow of Zarephath.

The Bible stipulates that while the earth remains, seed time and harvest, cold and heat, summer and winter, and day and night shall not cease. This typifies continuity of sowing and reaping in the life of the giver. It is wise not to allow seeding and sowing to cease with us, to establish unceasing harvest. Good seeds generate good harvest.

We see in Leviticus 1:3 and 3:1 how the Lord taught Israelites to do this. He stipulated how that the sacrifice they offer must be pleasant without flaw or blemish. "And the Lord had respect unto Abel and to his offering" (In Genesis 4:4).

By the act of giving, we meet needs that cause fulfilment, which in turn produces harvest. The Bible states that what a person sows, they shall reap and that God delights in a cheerful giver to reward them in good measure. By giving, self-centeredness and greed are dominated. What we give in to or invest in produces us harvest. You get blessed or are at advantage when you give to someone who is blessed. Your sowing will produce similar blessing. You may sow into something particular in someone because you want to attract the forcefield for such. Remember you are not looking to that person for that blessing, but the God who endows. It is the same when you invest your energy, resources, and time in a certain thing or area: sooner or later, you will reflect that to which you are dedicated. Because what you sow is what you reap, you attract the reward of your input. Tabitha (Dorcas) invested in the people, and her beneficiaries could not come to terms with her death; they fetched Peter, which consequentially brought her back to life (Acts 9:36–42).

Elisha's investments and dedication in serving Elijah accrued to him double portion of his master's anointing. The Shunammite woman's generous reaction to Elisha's need of accommodation resulted in recompense of a child she never had. Esther's response to the dilemma of the Jews saved her and her generation from annihilation. Obedient, timely reaction complements divine response order. Deborah the prophetess's corresponding action, not procrastinating another occasion to accompany Barak to battle, attributed to the victory.

God detests our procrastination to His command. When God gives us instructions, as obedient children, He expects our timely corresponding action. To delay is to disobey Him. To react at our own time and not His, is dishonor. Peter, Andrew, James, and John obeyed, following the Master straightaway (Matthew 4:18–22). Our promptness preserves, saves, and improves situations and circumstances, whether directly or indirectly.

Proverbs 19:17 (CEV) states, "Caring for the poor is lending to the Lord, and you will be well repaid," bearing in mind that God is a Rewarder of those who diligently seek Him with their substance. As you obey God's instructions and invest in His business of furthering the gospel through your support, sponsorship, faithful tithing, and helping the poor and needy through charity projects, His Word says that a multiplied harvest awaits you, and there won't be room enough to contain it. God gave Abraham the opportunity to sow, so he can reap His blessings. God provides us the opportunity to sow (investment in kingdom business) and earn a future of secured harvest. In essence, you secure divine commitment to His supply by your generosity.

If you have given to others, God causes other humans too to give back to you according to His Word in Luke 6:38. This may be through the caliber of job you'd secure, increased capital turnover or people's investment in your undertakings. However long it takes, the wind of harvest always locates the giver. Isaiah 41:21 enjoins us to produce our cause, meaning to justify why we are deserving of certain privileges. The priest's widow in 2 Kings 4:1–7 stated her case. "And thou knowest that thy servant did fear the Lord." A person who fears God does His will. If you have been sympathetic toward others, you can expect people to be generous toward you. "For whatsoever a man soweth, that shall he also reap" (Galatians 6:7).

A sower must be expectant of harvest just as a farmer will expect his crop to yield fruits. God sowed (gave up) His only begotten Son and reaped us as His harvest. God sacrificed heaven's best, portraying that giving does not have to be convenient. It is not stupidity to suffer inconvenience to bring about convenience for in others. Philippians 2:3 enjoins us to consider others above ourselves. Missionaries forsake their ease in pursuit of salvation and liberation of humanity as far as places where they are deprived basic comfort. Both the determination of the missionaries and their sponsors bring the divine deposit and deliverance witnessed to every human who is saved. When we are resolute about our sacrifice, purpose is facilitated—hence accomplishment of divine reward for the givers. Sowers are coexecutioners of divine plans and purposes. Due to their extraordinary role in kingdom expansion procedures, they fulfill divine design. They can be described as kingdom investors. "For where your treasure is, there will your heart be also" (Matthew 6:21).

God is the source and power behind giving. He engineers it. Giving is His nature. We are His vessels (conduits and channels) of all provisional respite. Earlier this morning before I sat to do my daily preview of this manuscript, God spontaneously brought to my memory a certain day in the past when He inquired of me to present certain precious items belonging to me to a parent in my children's school. It was challenging for me. You may want to ask, "How did you feel?" I'll be frank: the feeling wasn't great. But I knew better and obeyed. In honor and to His praise, I can proudly tell you that today, my result far outweighs and can never be compared to what I had to give up then. It's really humbling. This is a demonstration of Isaiah 55:9.

In 2009, by the leading of the Holy Spirit, I was instructed to give a monthly seed to a female minister despite having no financial income at all. This was when I had just quit secular employment for full-time ministry hinged on hope of God's guidance and provision. Committed to the instruction month in and month out, I posted my cheque to this lady from my residual income and savings from past paid employment. Later, it was this same minister who invited me to speak at a conference in the United States, where I met a young lady so passionate about what my ministry represents. Her support for me and ministry has been unequivocal; it can only be described as God at work. My sowing had paid off. Sowing has astonishing power. If you are sower, I congratulate you ahead of time.

Despite my need for revenue to facilitate the newly formed ministry assignment committed to me, I gave (sowed) relentlessly. Apostle Paul's words in Acts 20:35, "it is more blessed to give than to receive," was proven. I have now received so much in return. I can testify that my monthly seed then is bearing for me unbeatable harvest compared to the seed sowed. Sowing generates a chain reaction of blessings. By sowing, I gained the divine knowledge that giving it was not necessarily a subtraction but a factor for multiplication. Divine principle governs this act. It produces wisdom in any participators.

Reaping of harvest happens when obedience has been fulfilled: "They that sow in tears shall reap in joy" (Psalm 126:5). God's faithful reward is certain for doers of His Word. Our obedience to His Word is proof of our loyalty to Him. At times when we struggle to obey His Word, we must comfort ourselves with the assurance derivable in surrendering to God's will. Isaiah 26:3 states, "Thou wilt keep him in perfect peace, whose mind is stayed on thee: because he trusteth in thee."

Doing God's will is demonstration of trust in Him. The Bible enjoins us to give cheerfully because there is a guarantee of reward (2 Corinthians 9:6–8). As we comply with God's will regardless, we must remember that God's plans and thoughts for us are thoughts of good and not of evil, to give us to an expected end. God's Word in Proverbs 3:1 points us to obeying God and the reward of obedience in verse 4: "So shalt thou find favour and good understanding in the sight of God and man."

Generosity paves the way for the wise. His diligence to God's instruction propels him toward brighter future. The Bible states in Proverbs 22:29 that such a man's assiduity brings him before kings and not mean (ordinary) men. Like Joseph and Daniel, his steps are propelled toward favor and promotion. Proverbs 18:16 (NIV) tells us, "A gift opens the way and ushers the giver into the presence of the great."

The prudent will share and distribute. He will bless others out of His blessings and possession. He is sensitive to needs around him and meets such needs. He will serve God and people with his skill, knowledge, and substance. He wants to add value. He does not close his eyes to offering help to those around him—He responds to them, no matter how small he can offer, while seeking further assistance for them. Psalm 41:1 (NCV) tells us, "Happy are those who think about the poor. When trouble comes, the Lord will save them." Little wonder why certain people enjoy divine preservation in the midst of crises.

Commit to humane causes. Let your life count and matter beyond your immediate family. Give tithes, give offering, and join forces in meeting altruistic goals. Banish greed. Do not be like the self-centered man whom Jesus described in His parable found in Luke 12:15–21. Act wisely. The early Christians shared their possessions, and there was no lack amongst them (Acts 4:32). All the believers were of one heart and mind. No one claimed that any of their possessions was their own. We see in Acts 5 that Ananias and Sapphira, members of the early church family in Jerusalem, were rather greedy and dishonest who kept back what was theirs, and they suffered the consequence.

Matthew 6:19–21 admonishes us,

> Lay not up for yourselves treasures upon earth, where moth and rust doth corrupt, and where thieves break through and steal:

But lay up for yourselves treasures in heaven, where neither moth nor rust doth corrupt, and where thieves do not break through nor steal:

For where your treasure is, there will your heart be also.

Between 2011 and 2015, I witnessed how a lady, Agnes, was dedicated to an altruistic cause, which produced result for her. She was unrelenting through certain huddles, persisted, and gave her time and resources to make an impact. She was determined to see change and offered volunteer support for the organization. Her sacrifices were rather impressive. She was inciting a breakthrough by her investments and roles. I watched her through sacrifices that would inevitably lead to her turnaround change. Relentlessly in prayers, I pleaded a recompensing outcome for her and her family. Eventually, her harvest sought her out. She had provoked her desired change, and 2015 became unforgettable for her and her family, as well as for us members of CET-c for Women ministry. Agnes brought forth her change purposefully by her actions, sowing into God's work in the ministry. Her seeds had proved productive. The devil had to back off. Agnes played out Psalm 25:4–5, and she allowed God to show her, teach her, and lead her.

It is important that our hearts stay on God as our unfailing Source and Means. Being supply conscious that He is our Jehovah Jireh, God our Provider. Deprived circumstances must not cloud our perception of God. He is almighty and can make something out of nothing. Isaiah 55:8 tells us that His ways are far beyond our reasoning. Because His ways are distinct from ours, at times we do not quite understand it. The widow of Zarephath complied with God's will to give up all that was left to Elijah, and God's supply became unceasing for her (1 Kings 17:8–16). It may be a struggle, but sacrificial gestures done as act of kindness and in obedience to God's instruction, always yield recompense. They bring about the extraordinary (1 Kings 17:17–23). Timed harvest follows every act of benevolence. Seed time means a harvest time is sure. "For God is not unjust so as to forget your work and the love which you have shown for His name in ministering to [the needs of] the saints (God's people), as you do" (Hebrews 6:10 AMP). God is unfailing and faithful; He causes harvest that is commensurable to seed sown (2 Corinthians 9:6). The Bible tell us in Proverbs 11:25, "The liberal soul shall be made fat: and he that watereth shall be watered also himself."

Jeremiah 32:19 says of God, "Great in counsel, and mighty in work: for thine eyes are open upon all the ways of the sons of men: to give every one according to his ways, and according to the fruit of his doings." God gave Jesus. Jesus stopped at nothing to be the sacrifice that harvested us for God's redemption. We became the outcome of His death (seed sowed and buried). In Matthew 16:21–27 we read,

> From that time forth began Jesus to shew unto his disciples, how that he must go unto Jerusalem, and suffer many things of the elders and chief priests and scribes, and be killed, and be raised again the third day. Then Peter took him, and began to rebuke him, saying, Be it far from thee, Lord:

this shall not be unto thee. But he turned, and said unto Peter, Get thee behind me, Satan: thou art an offence unto me: for thou savourest not the things that be of God, but those that be of men. Then said Jesus unto his disciples, If any man will come after me, let him deny himself, and take up his cross, and follow me. For whosoever will save his life shall lose it: and whosoever will lose his life for my sake shall find it. For what is a man profited, if he shall gain the whole world, and lose his own soul? or what shall a man give in exchange for his soul? For the Son of man shall come in the glory of his Father with his angels; and then he shall reward every man according to his works.

Jesus demonstrated determination for the harvest of our souls. He stopped at nothing to ensure a harvesting and saving of our souls. He sowed His life in painful death that

He may bring forth fruits after His kind—people with His type of life and nature.

We are the outcome (harvest) of Christ's seed. The essence of our redemption today is Christ's giving. The Bible states in 1 John 4:17 "that as He is so are we," giving us His very nature—the nature of giving.

By His nature in us, we also bring others to Christ through the gesture of love, the nature of the Father in us. Willingness to give or share with others is a sign of generosity and liberty in our spirits. Ephesians 2:10 tells us that we are the workmanship of God in Christ created for good works. We are to follow His will in reaching out and caring for others. We, His children, are His means of physically reaching out to those who call on Him for help.

The act of giving and helping others are seed of good gestures that cause people to remember you, hold pleasing memory of you, pray for you and wish you well. The Bible states that a person's gift makes room for him and associate him with people that matter (Proverbs 18:16). Total reliance on God's direction channels us into God's blessings and provisions. We must not look to those we have helped or see them as obligated to us. No matter who they are, they cannot reward us perfectly like God. "It is better to trust in the Lord than to put confidence in man" (Psalm 118:8). If you have sowed, you will reap; be patient for God's timing. His recompense comes at the best occasion because He makes all things beautiful in His time (Ecclesiastes 3:11).

God expects us to give with discernment. We cannot give what we do not have, or offer what we do not possess. Neither can we deliver what God has not empowered us to deliver. The widow of Zarephath ascertained that Elijah was truly a man of God. Her action was based on discernment of God's will. The Bible warns in 1 John 4:1 (ESV) to test all spirits (i.e., cross-check, re-examine, and be sure). "Beloved, do not believe every spirit, but test the spirits to see whether they are from God, for many false prophets have gone out into the world."

First Timothy 6:18 (NLT) instructs us, "Tell them to use their money to do good. They should be rich in good works and generous to those in need, always being ready to share with others." God expects us to reach out to the needy amongst us and not close our eyes to their plights. When we show sympathy or say we empathize, and we say we care or are our brothers' keepers, we must ensure that our actions match our words. God expects us to be humane even toward those who are against us (Matthew 5:43–47). Therefore, in His true nature, we reach out not just to those who have not offended us. Jesus said in Luke 6:31 (NLT), "Do to others as you would like them to do to you."

I read of a man who requested His son-in-law build him a house in the city where he lived with his daughter. Instead of the young man giving his best, he used low-quality materials, and the house was of low standard. He was self-centered and inconsiderate, and never was anyone's progression or achievement his interest. He was unperturbed about the poor-quality job. On completion, he told his father-in-law that the work was done. His wife's father thanked him, announcing to him that he planned a house of the couple's choice as a gift because he wanted to meet their taste, and the best way was to ask his son-in-law to build the house under the pretext that it was for him and then present the house to them as a couple. The young man regretted not lavishing time and effort in building a state-of-the-art house for his father-in-law as if building for a king. He short-changed himself and his wife. He knew his father-in-law could afford a quality mansion even in a best part of the city, but he was narrow-minded and too self-involved. He did not sow or invest his efforts, hence he did not reap a profitable harvest. People say what goes around comes around. This is proved positive through the aftermath of this man's insensitivity and inconsiderateness. God does not want us insensitive to others; He wants us to be mindful and caring, asking us to love and treat our neighbors as ourselves. "'Love your neighbor as yourself.' There is no commandment greater" (Mark 12:31 NIV).

If you are mindful of others, God is mindful of you. A child of God will live the life Jesus lived by His good deeds in honor to the Father (Acts 10:38). For us to say that we truly serve God, our love and loyalty to Him must be portrayed through our deeds. James 1:27

(NLT) states, "Pure and genuine religion in the sight of God the Father means caring for orphans and widows in their distress and refusing to let the world corrupt you." Let people trace your sacrifice to the nature of God in you. Philippians 2:3 tells us, "Do nothing out of selfish ambition or vain conceit. Rather, in humility value others above yourselves." Fill your life with God's nature because what you do not have, you cannot give.

The offspring of God, because of the inherent nature of their Father, derives pleasure in giving of their substance to needs around them. Exodus 35:29 states, "The children of Israel brought a willing offering unto the Lord, every man and woman, whose heart made them willing to bring for all manner of work, which the Lord had commanded to be made by the hand of Moses." As Abraham's descendants, they recognize that increase in wealth or its enhancement is through the act of generosity. They sustain their blessings through sacrificial regeneration and showing obligation to the needy amongst them.

The early Christians followed suit, and they engaged in daily distribution of food and other essentials to the world around them. Your immediate environment is your own world. What is the contribution you can make there? Deliberately make impact. Do not say there is nothing for you to add. Simply look inward and get something out to your world. Your world needs you. You are the answer to someone's riddle. It is a great thing to be a response to a plight. God is counting on you as His channel to meet a need. Revelation 22:12, says, "And, behold, I come quickly; and my reward is with me, to give every man according as his work shall be."

People come together in collaboration as partners to sponsor a cause for united effort and strength. This is one way in which God has promoted the work of CET-c for Women, which serves as an answer and response to prayers for marital effectiveness and the rescue of homes and families in marital crises. God never forgets but pays due diligence in recompensing these ministry partners. I have witnessed His trend in blessing their undertakings from one level of glory to another. The Bible alleges in Psalms

35:27, "Let them shout for joy, and be glad, that favour my righteous cause: yea, let them say continually, Let the LORD be magnified, which hath pleasure in the prosperity of his servant." When we are faithful and committed to His cause, He is faithful to us. Proverbs 11:25 (NIV) states, "A generous person will prosper; whoever refreshes others will be refreshed." Make up your mind to release or share with others what you have. Your determination brings about divine deposit and deliverance. Heaven backs you up, and you are delivered from lack consciousness into a life of supply consciousness (Philippians 4:19). The Psalmist says, "I have been young, and now am old; yet have I not seen the righteous forsaken, nor his seed begging bread" (Psalm 37:25). Simply do what is appropriate and do not compromise, because this is how character is built.

On most occasions, there is usually a waiting period before reaping. Nevertheless, harvest is certain for the diligent and cheerful giver. God gives power to get wealth (Deuteronomy 8:18). Disobedience and doubt hinder progress. When Peter observed the waves, he began to sink (Matthew 14:28–30). Reflecting on the case of the retiree who said she was led to offer a certain amount to me, she did not observe her retiree status, but considered God faithful to replenish her. Years later, she enjoys a monthly proceed from me as equally led. Wow! This is straight outcome of obedience and sowing. Indeed, whatever we do for others, we have in one way or another done it for ourselves. It was while writing this book that the Holy Spirit enlightened me that it all started at the point when she took the step to sow that seed years ago. Even if I had forgotten the gesture, but God did not! My view is that when God asks us to do anything, even if we don't understand it, we should let the fact that it is to a noble cause motivate us, and just do it gladly considering that we a hope of harvest. "God loves a cheerful giver" (2 Corinthians 9:7).

If you think what you have is little, and you refuse to sow, you may be restricting yourself. It is wise to challenge yourself into an unprecedented future harvest. Such harvest may show up as saving grace in dire times in kind or cash when you need it the most. They meet unique demand because divine principles apply to them.

Even if it's to circumvent mediocrity, sowing is well worth the price and sacrifice. Saying to yourself that you have nothing to share with others but little, just for yourself alone, is not the way to increase what you have. Share with others, and you will find help in time of need. I will say still sow to provoke the harvest of much. Invest in what meets a need, however small. Make your life count. Be intentional about sowing and giving and in due course, our seeds will find you out.

Avoid living a self-centered life. Break the curse of selfishness and stinginess. Some have been oblivious and unwary of this vice and evil, that it degenerated to being selfish and stingy towards their own self. Don't deprive yourself and others! Be a giver. Whatever your situation is, it is not indicative of the blessing you can still be to others in whatever way, form, or shape possible. Just be a blessing. Whatever you invest in others either in gift or gesture invariably serves to become investment for your future need.

Sacrifices are what you give up for the benefit of another. When a needy person prays to God, God will reveal to His own, the sheep of His pasture (Psalm 100:3), who hears His voice (John 10:27), and goes into action to do His will.

He serves as God's stretched-out hands and he gets God's attention for serving. This is the way God's special favor is accrued. God's blessings follow the giver (Proverbs 19:17, 22:9 GNT). The Bible assures that the gift and sacrifice of such a person promotes him (Psalm 112:9; Proverbs 18:16). The fruit of Joseph's seed (interpretation of the butler's dream) though took a while, eventually took Joseph from prison to the palace, and he became the prime minister in a foreign land, Egypt. He ensued the unimaginable, by protocols broken in his favor. Mordecai raised Esther to be obedient, God-fearing, and well disciplined, and the fruit was that Esther preserved Mordecai and her fellow Jews from annihilation. Sooner or later, your own fruits and harvest will show up too. Keep doing the Father's will, giving quality seeds, and engaging in Kingdom endeavors. We know that the nature and quality of seed determines the nature and category of harvest. The nature of harvest is either for a season (one-off) or continuous and perpetual. Perfect seed results in perfect harvest. Jeremiah 32:19 stipulates, "For thine eyes are open upon all the ways of the sons of men: to give everyone according to his ways, and according to the fruit of his doings."

Financial gesture is not the only way by which we can add value to people or our immediate world. By continued and deliberate improvement on our inherent abilities, we can aim at pleasing God. God made each of us with special qualities by which we can be a blessing to our world. Joseph and Daniel exacted their special qualities and ability by interpretation of dreams that eventually set them up for recognition. "Seest thou a man diligent in his business? he shall stand before kings; he shall not stand before mean men" (Proverbs 22:29). Don't allow any unpleasantness of the past deprive you of impending opportunities. In relationships and in our dealings with fellow humans, the tells us to sow love, joy, and peace, patience, kindness, goodness, faithfulness, gentleness, and self-control (Galatians 5:22-23). When we demonstrate these qualities, providence is inevitable.

Be found doing God's will, like Isaac. According to God's instruction, he stayed and sowed in Gerar, a land devastated by famine, and he prospered (Genesis 26:1–6, 12–14). After having obeyed God, there was God's supernatural increase for Isaac. In 2 Corinthians 1:20, the Bible states that God's promises are backed by yes and amen, meaning it is unfailing and certainly comes to pass.

You can't be selfish and be happy, but a generous heart is merry. He is constantly refreshed (Proverbs 11:25). God's Word in John 16:24 conveys to us to ask so that we may receive and so that our joy may be full. But if you have not been giving, you may not be able to confidently and boldly command divine supplies. In Luke 6:38, the Bible tells us, "Give, and it shall be given unto you; good measure, pressed down, and shaken together, and running over, shall men give into your bosom. For with the same measure that ye mete withal it shall be measured to you again." This scripture promises that when you give and release to others, more generous giving returns to us. Second Corinthians 9:6 portrays God's responses and promises in the form of a bountiful harvest that follows bountiful sowing. God is faithful to His Word (1 Thessalonians 5:24). Giving is a spiritual duty, a calling that God rewards beyond comprehension (Ephesians 3:20). For those who choose to be selfish, James 2:13 (NLT) states, "There will be no mercy for those who have not shown mercy to others."

Christ, our example, lived a life of selflessness and generosity to others. The Bible points to how Jesus, anointed with the Holy Ghost and power, was consistent in doing good and healing all those oppressed of the devil (Acts 10:38). Friends, following His footsteps, let us also serve by doing good. Has God anointed you with power, influence, better opportunities, and position than others? I commend you to do good with it just like Jesus.

We see Paul's selflessness toward kingdom endeavour (Acts 20:20, 24). He was sold out to the gospel and could not be stopped. He ensured he lived a life that was beneficial to others. Apostle Paul enjoins us to be examples to our world: "Be their ideal; let them follow the way you teach and live; be a pattern for them in your love, your faith, and your clean thoughts" (1 Timothy 4:12 TLB). He asks us to be of benefit to others from what God has blessed us with. When we do this, we make room for increased provision (Proverbs 11:25).

I watched a young lady care so much by being a blessing to God's work and His minister. Week in and week out, with excitement, she provides assistance that serves to relieve the minister's workload. Despite being a low-income earner, she was convinced that the duties were hers to undertake. She had the conviction and was self-driven. A few years down the line, she found herself in Australia. She called to tell me out of the blue one day that every single investment made in England turned out as an opportunity and a means to dreams realized in a foreign land. She had sowed in England, and she is now reaping in far Australia. She termed it as a prophet's reward, referencing Matthew 10:41.

As our lives flow to others as streams of God's blessing, God in turn supplies our need (Philippians 4:19). We must not hold anything so dear beyond God, the Giver of the gifts. His Kingdom advancement must be our priority. Genesis 4:4 says, "And the Lord had respect unto Abel and to his offering." Abel acknowledged God above his earnings. Regardless of what we earn, we must always remember to give some in acknowledgement of the Giver, to further His cause of salvation of the souls of humans, which brings rewarding blessings. (Psalm 35:27).

As God's children, we have this nature of the Father who is kind to both the deserving and the undeserving.

> If you love only the people who love you, what praise should you get? Even sinners love the people who love them. If you do good only to those who do good to you, what praise should you get? Even sinners do that! If you lend things to people, always hoping to get something back, what praise should you get? Even sinners lend to other sinners so that they can get back the same amount! But love your enemies, do good to

them, and lend to them without hoping to get anything back. Then you will have a great reward, and you will be children of the Most High God, because he is kind even to people who are ungrateful and full of sin. Show mercy, just as your Father shows mercy. (Luke 6:32–36 (NCV)

# Chapter 5

# The Essence

Giving amounts to receiving. It warrants the expectation of greater measure of returns (Ephesians 3:20) which comes in its due season. These returns serve as God's blessings for what is sowed in obedience to His will. Based on the above scripture, the reward is far greater and very rewarding, and the result is longer lasting than what could have been sowed. Giving and receiving are components in God's promotion plan. Giving is a personal decision that requires sacrifice of personal resources: our time, finances, comfort, and energy etc. God honors sacrificial giving deprived of acting like a martyr (Matthew 6:4).

Our intrinsic God character causes us to be distributors of blessings. God's desire is that we prosper and profit (3 John 2). He points us to how to profit (Isaiah 48:17) through giving. The Bible state in First Timothy 5:18 that the laborer deserves reward. The givers labors to give joy, hope, and peace to the receiver and in like manner, the giver derives same along God's increase and blessings of abundance as recompense for his action. Sowing and receiving brings about fulfilment in a mutual way for giver and receiver alike.

I remember during one of my ministry's annual retreat conference. On the finishing day, a minister who had come as participant from the Middle East walked up to me and said the Lord told her to donate a box of her published book. Prior to our reunion at the conference hall that morning, I was unsure whether to share and dialogue with her over a strange revelation and sensitive encounter I had overnight regarding her. I was awed and touched by her obligation to the Holy Spirit and her act of benevolence. Her action incited the release and my opening up for her advantage. With sense of commitment, confidence, and relief, I recounted the encounter to her. Inspired within my spirit, I made declarations and prayer pronunciations as the Lord gave me utterances over the matter.

One afternoon later that month, I was reading a copy of the book, and it turned out to be such a blessing, so much so that I heard the Lord say, "Sow into the writer's life." There and then, I called to ask for her bank account details to plant my seed. The outcome of my seed was a beautiful new door to publishing for me and my ministry. The Bible states in Proverbs 11:25, "The liberal soul shall be made fat: and he that watereth shall be watered also himself."

God provides the jobs, our means of income, which serves as the avenue of God's supply. Our job is not our source. God is our source, our hope and stay (focus). Philippians 4:19 tells us that according to His riches, He supplies our needs. Therefore, when we give, God is faithful to replenish the giver in good measure (Luke 6:38). In Matthew 7:11–12, Jesus portrays God's willingness to supply our needs.

> If ye then, being evil, know how to
> give good gifts unto your children,

how much more shall your Father which is in heaven give good things to them that ask him? Therefore all things whatsoever ye would that men should do to you, do ye even so to them: for this is the law and the prophets.

Trust God today. He can do far beyond our imaginations (Ephesians 3:20).

Defeat the stronghold of selfishness and self-centeredness. Resist lack consciousness. Be supply conscious like apostle Paul, who reassured himself, "God will supply according to His riches in glory by Christ Jesus" (Philippians 4:19). God's supply is guaranteed to those who give to others. Give out of your plenty, and give even out of your few. When we do the extraordinary, we get the extraordinary. Giving does not have to be convenient. The Bible tells us that those who go weeping bearing precious seed will doubtless come back with rejoicing. "They go out weeping, carrying seed for sowing, and return singing, carrying their sheaves" (Psalm 126:6 TLB). There will be payback.

By doing good for others, you discover later that you did yourself good. This is my personal experience and what I have witnessed in those who have helped around me. God has diverse ways of rewarding our acts of blessing. Deeds of blessing to others—big or small; in the form of care, love, or affection; even as simple as a smile, an encouraging act, or support and motivation for others— are beautiful gestures that bear fruits for the giver.

God's nature in us His children must at all times portray the fruits of the Spirit (an effect or offshoot of God's Spirit in us), which are love, joy, peace, patience, kindness, faithfulness, goodness, gentleness, and self-control, according to Galatians 5:22–23. Make determined giving. Our God is Jehovah Jireh, the Great Provider. David stated in Psalm 23:1, "The Lord is my shepherd; I shall not want." He declares that God is his Source!

Cognizant of their God, the Israelites were indiscriminate (Exodus 35:21–29). Do you know your God? Then meet feasible needs around you. God's blessings never run out on His kids. Be supply conscious; your heavenly Father is God of "more than enough," God of miracles, God of wonders, God of all possibilities and God of provision. In 2 Corinthians 8:9 the Bible states, "For ye know the grace of our Lord Jesus Christ, that, though he was rich, yet for your sakes he became poor, that ye through his poverty might be rich."

God's Word equips us for propagative blessings. Giving is a simple principle guiding proliferation and multiplication. Think about the participant from Middle East who donated a box of her published book to my ministry, and how God later guided me to making personal investment in her work. Likewise, how my obedient action translated to fulfilling my own publishing requirement. Indeed, whatever good you do to others; you have done it for yourself, one way or another. The amazing effect of giving is a ripple effect of manifold blessings.

Truly, our giving reproduces. Today, I am the effect of investment and labor of the earlier missionaries. Their investments are still reproducing effects beyond their seed and existence. Indeed, God's Word is enduring.

Prayers are answered when we do God's bidding of meeting needs presented to Him in prayer. Inevitably God's recompense and augmented blessings ensues for each "vessels" that has served as God's means to others.

> And God is able to make all grace [every favor and earthly blessing] come in abundance to you, so that you may always [under all circumstances, regardless of the need] have complete sufficiency in everything [being completely self-sufficient in Him], and have an abundance for every good work and act of charity. As it is written and forever remains written, "He [the benevolent and generous person] scattered abroad, he gave to the poor, His righteousness endures forever!" Now He who provides seed for the sower and bread for food will provide and multiply your seed for

sowing [that is, your resources] and increase the harvest of your righteousness [which shows itself in active goodness, kindness, and love]. You will be enriched in every way so that you may be generous, and this [generosity, administered] through us is producing thanksgiving to God [from those who benefit]. (2 Corinthians 9:8–11)

Giving has the giver at these advantages. It opens the giver up for unprecedented blessings and capacity. Giving generates wisdom and understanding in the giver. According to Proverbs 24:3, "Through wisdom a house is built and by understanding it is established." In essence, for the giver, what takes effect is wisdom and insightfulness due to divine principle, "generosity begets generosity".

Matthew 5:16 says, "Let your light so shine before men, that they may see your good works, and glorify your Father which is in heaven."

## *Keynote*

- God is our source, not our job or our bank account.
- Be supply conscious, not lack conscious.
- Be subject to God and the Holy Spirit, not your finances. Allow God's instruction to guide your giving, not your financial state.
- Don't place worldly discretion above divine principles.
- "The earth belongs to God! Everything in all the world is His" (Psalm 24:1 TLB).
- Sow by faith and not by sensory perception.
- Break the cycle of lack through deliberate giving.
- Your sacrifice will unleash unparalleled outcomes.
- There is no one in life with nothing. A simple smile where desirable can evoke change. It only has to be deliberate. Find a need and meet it.

# Conclusion

God's Word says in Genesis 8:22, "While the earth remaineth, seedtime and harvest, and cold and heat, and summer and winter, and day and night shall not cease."

The world's inhabitants must conform to the way God has designed it to function. He created the earth to receive seed and invariably produce harvest. This law governs proliferation, just as day and night, summer and winter alternate without fail, so must seed time and harvest be unfailing. Because a seed yields after itself in multiples, so we must keep sowing for replenishment and increase.

This is God's Word in Psalms 112:3–9 for the sower.

Wealth and riches shall be in his house: and his righteousness endureth for ever. Unto the upright there ariseth light in the darkness: he is gracious, and full of compassion, and righteous. A good man sheweth favour, and lendeth: he will guide his affairs with discretion. Surely he shall not be moved for ever: the righteous shall be in everlasting remembrance. He shall not be afraid of evil tidings: his heart is fixed, trusting in the Lord. His heart is established, he shall not be afraid, until he see his desire upon his enemies. He hath dispersed, he hath given to the poor; his righteousness endureth for ever; his horn shall be exalted with honour.

This describes the sower. Through giving, he pleases the Lord, making His will be done on earth. He facilitates God's desire and therefore blessed. He is a partaker of Abrahamic blessings (Galatians 3:29 TLB).

Abraham passed God's test. He proved unselfish in surrendering Isaac to God. He did not hold back the gift (Isaac) from the Giver (God). He acknowledged God as the Source of his having Isaac and was not foolish to withhold him from the Giver. Genesis 14:14–24 portrays Abraham as neither greedy nor materialistic. Abraham displayed contentment and integrity. Not greedy, he gave a tenth of everything he earned to Priest Melchizedek (Genesis 14:20 and Hebrews 7:1-2). His hoped of harvest was God, who is being served. He was certain that God is no person's debtor for a recompense. Hebrews 6:10 (NIV) tells us, "God is not unjust; he will not forget your work and the love you have shown him as you have helped his people and continue to help them."

In due season, our harvest finds us out. It always locates us. After Jonathan's death, the harvest of his seed of good gesture and love to David emerged and was reaped even in his son Mephibosheth (2 Samuel 9:1–7). Abraham's charitable gesture to strangers (Genesis 18:1–14) translated to unceasing generational blessings from Isaac to Jacob/ Israel to this present day. The fruitage of his selflessness and altruism are rewards that outlast him (Genesis 13:5–11, 22:1–18).

Certain possessions held dear by people several years back that they could not part with are now in the junkyard, lacking in value. Many have had bad experiences with loved ones because they were unable to part with so-called costly items that today are worth nothing. This wasn't Abraham's case. He spared the good and rich land to Lot and earned blessings. He realized he never lost after all (Genesis 13:1–17). Givers don't lack. They will always have the edge. Christ's Word, quoted in Acts 20:35, says, "It is more blessed to give than to receive." The giver leaves worthy impression on the receiver. The benefactor's deed naturally induces the goodwill of the beneficiary. They are wished well, prayed for, loved and appreciated, and especially wanted around for longer, as seen in Tabitha's case (Acts 9:36–41). Psalm 90:12 says to ask God to teach us to apply our hearts to wisdom. It inspires us to do what we must do in timely to have a head start in life. It is better to be spirit-led rather than live life based on things that perish or are transient (1 John 2:15–17).

Our harvest will find us out in due time if we have been sowing. Seeing a need and meeting it is satisfying the will of God (Isaiah 58:7–12). Paul the apostle said that no eye has seen, no ear has heard, and no human mind has ever conceived the things God has prepared for those who love Him, who prove it by doing His will (1 Corinthians 2:9).

In 2008, I was at a women's conference in Boston. One afternoon while in worship and praying to the Lord in the hotel room where I lodged, lo and behold, I heard God say to involve a particular gentleman at church I pastored at the time, in monthly giving subscription to my upcoming charity. I was taken aback because the charity is apparently designated to women, even from its name: CET-c for Women. The challenge was, "How do I present such to a man? How does this relate to him? Why? How, God? What is this all about, Lord?" These were the questions that raced through my mind as I prayed and finished up to digest this new task. I was worried and felt bound and compelled to follow the instruction given. I knew this was God and knew there was no escaping or shirking from this directive. Distinctively, it was an order from above.

To my surprise, God had prepared this man. Up till date he is still supporting the assignment of the charity which is to foment marriage stability and family cohesion. It was nearly ten years later, and I became privy to God's plan for instructing his involvement in a marriage ministry. God had reminded me that his wife had hinted to me in the past of a plan to quietly walk out of their marriage.

This man's seed in a marriage ministry has been the saving link. What a privilege to witness his harvest of marital bliss. Wow! God's wisdom! "O the depth of the riches both of the wisdom and knowledge of God! how unsearchable are his judgments, and his ways past finding out!" (Romans 11:33).

The struggle that almost crippled this marriage has since been crippled by faithful sowing. What the giver is making possible for others, God makes possible for him. "What goes around comes around" is true and proved positive by the power of seed.

# Thus Saith the Spirit

"The life of a giver is a life of an overcomer."

## Call to His Saving Grace

You are in God's plan. You are not an accident. He is your Maker. He offers reunion with you today. For God so loves you that He gave up heaven's best in the person of Jesus Christ (John 3:16) that you may be restored to Him.

The Bible tells us in John 3:3 that unless we are born of God (born again), we have no part with Him. Therefore, be born of the God for the fullness of life only available in Him.

Now is your time of salvation. Ask God, in the person of Jesus Christ to come, be the Lord of your life.

Therefore, make the following statement below but mean it with all your heart.

> Lord Jesus, thank You for your sacrifice for me. I surrender my life to You. Now I have a brand-new life. I am child of God. I am born again.
>
> Amen.

Congratulations, you just did it! You are now a member of God's family.

To learn how to grow your faith or find answers to questions you may have, watch *Pastor Bim TV*, a daily inspiration on YouTube, to enhance your daily walk with God.

You can also contact Pastor Bim and her ministry, CET-c For Women.

Website: www.cet-c4women.org
Email: info@cet-c4women.org
Phone: +44 7540499191
Instagram: @cet-cforwomen
Twitter: @cet-cforwomen

Printed in the United States
by Baker & Taylor Publisher Services